Redis Applied Design Patterns

Use Redis' features to enhance your software development through a wide range of practical design patterns

Arun Chinnachamy

BIRMINGHAM - MUMBAI

Redis Applied Design Patterns

First published: September 2014

Production reference: 1160914

Published by Packt Publishing Ltd.
Livery Place
35 Livery Street
Birmingham B3 2PB, UK.

ISBN 978-1-78328-671-3

www.packtpub.com

Credits

Author
Arun Chinnachamy

Reviewers
Thorsten Böttger
Chad Lung
Andrea Pavoni
Jaspal Singh

Commissioning Editor
Pramila Balan

Acquisition Editors
Nikhil Chinnari
Kevin Colaco

Content Development Editor
Arvind Koul

Technical Editor
Ankita Thakur

Copy Editors
Janbal Dharmaraj
Stuti Srivastava

Project Coordinators
Neha Bhatnagar
Melita Lobo

Proofreaders
Simran Bhogal
Bernadette Watkins

Indexer
Hemangini Bari

Production Coordinator
Komal Ramchandani

Cover Work
Komal Ramchandani

About the Author

Arun Chinnachamy is a developer and systems architect who focuses on building software applications. He is a multifaceted programmer who has gained experience in multiple technologies and programming languages over the years, ranging from ADA and C# to PHP.

Currently, he works as the technology head at MySmartPrice, one of the leading online shopping discovery platforms in India.

I would like to express my gratitude to the great minds that created Redis and made available this exciting piece of software as open source.

This work would not have been possible without the support of my parents and my wife, Suvarchala, and my son, Aadith, who are patient with my round-the-clock working hours.

I would like to thank the open source community for excellent documentation about Redis, which was of incredible help during my early days with Redis, and my special thanks goes to Harish.

It is totally unfair not to thank my editor and publisher who believed in me and provided this excellent opportunity to share my experience with you.

I would also like to thank each and every person who helped me to develop my skills over the years and helped me to find the best in myself.

About the Reviewers

Thorsten Böttger is a senior software developer from Hamburg, Germany. He loves coding in all kinds of languages, mainly using Ruby. Besides that, he speaks at conferences about his work, plays the guitar, and also enjoys photography. He loves coffee and talking about geography and history.

Thorsten has worked on many projects in Germany and New Zealand, from start-ups to enterprises, and sometimes spiking (tiny) projects as well. He and his team have won the Rails Rumble award for the Most Useful Application in 2010.

He has reviewed various books in the past, covering topics such as Java, Spring, Hibernate, and Ruby on Rails.

> I would like to thank my kids and especially my wife for giving me the time and the support to do all the stuff I'm thinking of.

Chad Lung is a cloud engineer in the EMC Rubicon Cloud Services Group. Currently, he is an active OpenStack contributor and has over 17 years of industry experience in various roles.

Originally born in Canada, he moved to the United States in 1997 and began his software engineering career with full force. He has worked with various technologies and with large cloud-based companies such as Rackspace and EMC.

Chad has three boys and lives with his wife in San Antonio, Texas.

Andrea Pavoni is a passionate Italian programmer. He's mostly focused on web and mobile development, always looking for the best tools available. In his 15-year career, Andrea has had the opportunity to work in several IT fields such as governments and big company brands.

Andrea currently works at Cantiere Creativo, a 12-year-old Florentine company, an agile-oriented web agency and partner in various start-ups.

Sometimes, Andrea posts on his blog and loves to experiment with new tools and languages, releasing them as open source whenever possible. He is also an active member of the Italian Ruby community. He has helped in the organization of past Ruby Day editions and also coached at the first Italian Rails Girls event in Rome.

Jaspal Singh is a technology evangelist with decades of professional experience in the IT sector. Jaspal has hands-on as well as strategic-level experience of working on the latest leading-edge technologies such as PHP, Solr, Redis, Node.js, and MongoDB.

Jaspal has also been a fairly active tech entrepreneur with engagements in many web applications and portals. In his spare time, Jaspal likes to read and keep abreast of the latest technologies and trends in the IT space.

Jaspal has expertise in building enterprise scale applications with high availability and scalable real-time production systems delivering high performance.

Jaspal can be added as professional contact on `http://www.linkedin.com/in/jsxtech` and you may e-mail him at `jsxtech@gmail.com`.

www.PacktPub.com

Support files, eBooks, discount offers, and more

You might want to visit www.PacktPub.com for support files and downloads related to your book.

Did you know that Packt offers eBook versions of every book published, with PDF and ePub files available? You can upgrade to the eBook version at www.PacktPub.com and as a print book customer, you are entitled to a discount on the eBook copy. Get in touch with us at service@packtpub.com for more details.

At www.PacktPub.com, you can also read a collection of free technical articles, sign up for a range of free newsletters and receive exclusive discounts and offers on Packt books and eBooks.

http://PacktLib.PacktPub.com

Do you need instant solutions to your IT questions? PacktLib is Packt's online digital book library. Here, you can access, read and search across Packt's entire library of books.

Why subscribe?

- Fully searchable across every book published by Packt
- Copy and paste, print and bookmark content
- On demand and accessible via web browser

Free access for Packt account holders

If you have an account with Packt at www.PacktPub.com, you can use this to access PacktLib today and view nine entirely free books. Simply use your login credentials for immediate access.

Table of Contents

Preface

The computing world is changing fast. In this fast-moving environment, there is no choice other than to deliver data quickly to the user. Every day there are new innovations poured into the market, and it is important to make effective use of them in our application. Redis is one of the fastest data stores out in the market, which is being used by giants in the web industry. However, to add Redis into your stack, it needs a different level of thinking.

Understanding Redis is only part of the learning curve; as engineers, it is critical to understand various techniques that are necessary to use the features of Redis effectively. The main goal of the book is to help you design applications using various data structures in Redis. This book focuses on how to use Redis in real-life situations with live examples.

What this book covers

Chapter 1, *The SQL and NoSQL Way*, focuses on changes in thought processes required to work with NoSQL solutions in comparison with a SQL relational system.

Chapter 2, *Transactions and Locks*, explains transactions in Redis and how the data locking mechanism works in Redis.

Chapter 3, *Data Types in Redis*, helps you understand various data types available in Redis and when to use each of them.

Chapter 4, *Redis as a Caching Server*, shows you how to use Redis as a simple caching server in a matter of minutes. This chapter also explains how to take advantage of special encoding in Redis to optimize the cache size.

Chapter 5, *Redis in an E-commerce Inventory System*, explains various areas of an e-commerce site where Redis can be used to make things faster.

Chapter 6, Redis in Autosuggest, describes how Redis can be used as a backend system for simple faceting and as an autosuggest system to make the system ultrafast.

Chapter 7, Redis in Real-time Analysis, describes how to use Redis for operational intelligence and real-time analysis. It helps you understand how to make use of Redis to gather some important information to make decisions in real time.

Chapter 8, Redis in Gaming, explains how Redis can be used to store player data and how pub/sub can be used to implement player chats.

Chapter 9, Redis in a Commenting System, describes Redis as a backend for managing types of content such as comments.

Chapter 10, Redis in Advertising Networks, describes why Redis is suitable for implementing a fast ad network and shows you how to design an ad inventory system.

Chapter 11, Redis in Social Networks, describes how Redis can be used as a backend for social network features such as news feeds and notifications.

What you need for this book

In order to make your learning more effective, you need a computer with any flavor of Linux, preferably Ubuntu or Debian, installed. Redis is not production ready in Windows, so Linux is preferred to try various design patterns in Redis.

Also, you'll need a suitable development environment for your favorite language in order to try some use cases. Familiarity with relational database systems will be helpful. Most of the examples in this book contain PHP code, so the ability to understand the code is essential to make the most out of the book.

Who this book is for

This book is for developers and/or system architects who are already proficient in programming and traditional database systems and want to learn how to use Redis to design and build scalable, fast applications. This book does not cover how to install and configure Redis and assumes the reader is already proficient with the basics of Redis.

Conventions

In this book, you will find a number of styles of text that distinguish between different kinds of information. Here are some examples of these styles, and an explanation of their meaning.

Code words in text, database table names, folder names, filenames, file extensions, pathnames, dummy URLs, user input, and Twitter handles are shown as follows: "In the preceding scenario, if there is an error in the second query, the user is not deleted from the tbl_students table."

A block of code is set as follows:

```
BEGIN TRANSACTION;
DELETE FROM tbl_students WHERE user_id='3';
DELETE FROM tbl_student_subjects WHERE user_id='3';
COMMIT;
```

Any command-line input or output is written as follows:

```
HMSET JOHN subject1 Math subject2 Biology
HMSET SMITH subject1 Math subject2 Physics
HMSET SCOTT subject1 Biology
```

New terms and **important words** are shown in bold.

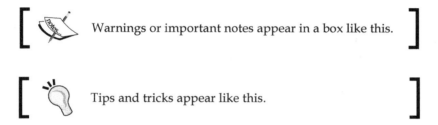

Warnings or important notes appear in a box like this.

Tips and tricks appear like this.

Reader feedback

Feedback from our readers is always welcome. Let us know what you think about this book—what you liked or may have disliked. Reader feedback is important for us to develop titles that you really get the most out of.

To send us general feedback, simply send an e-mail to feedback@packtpub.com, and mention the book title via the subject of your message.

If there is a topic that you have expertise in and you are interested in either writing or contributing to a book, see our author guide on www.packtpub.com/authors.

Customer support

Now that you are the proud owner of a Packt book, we have a number of things to help you to get the most from your purchase.

Downloading the example code

You can download the example code files for all Packt books you have purchased from your account at http://www.packtpub.com. If you purchased this book elsewhere, you can visit http://www.packtpub.com/support and register to have the files e-mailed directly to you.

Errata

Although we have taken every care to ensure the accuracy of our content, mistakes do happen. If you find a mistake in one of our books—maybe a mistake in the text or the code—we would be grateful if you would report this to us. By doing so, you can save other readers from frustration and help us improve subsequent versions of this book. If you find any errata, please report them by visiting http://www.packtpub. com/submit-errata, selecting your book, clicking on the **errata submission form** link, and entering the details of your errata. Once your errata are verified, your submission will be accepted and the errata will be uploaded on our website, or added to any list of existing errata, under the Errata section of that title. Any existing errata can be viewed by selecting your title from http://www.packtpub.com/support.

Piracy

Piracy of copyright material on the Internet is an ongoing problem across all media. At Packt, we take the protection of our copyright and licenses very seriously. If you come across any illegal copies of our works, in any form, on the Internet, please provide us with the location address or website name immediately so that we can pursue a remedy.

Please contact us at copyright@packtpub.com with a link to the suspected pirated material.

We appreciate your help in protecting our authors, and our ability to bring you valuable content.

Questions

You can contact us at questions@packtpub.com if you are having a problem with any aspect of the book, and we will do our best to address it.

1
The SQL and NoSQL Way

Databases play a vital role in our life. Almost every application relies on a database for its operation. A database could be a flat file with a few bytes of data or a more complex system holding petabytes of data. Designing a database model is essential for an application to work effectively. Since the dawn of database systems, SQL databases ruled this technology space. SQL databases work on a relational database model that uses a tabular structure in which each element has a defined relationship with the other. However, recently, new generations of NoSQL databases have been created to combat the rising demands of data, and they are seeing widespread adoption from both technology giants and startups alike. This new wave of NoSQL databases has created a new school of thought, which requires a radically different thought process when compared to SQL databases.

This chapter explores the major differences between SQL and NoSQL databases, and provides an insight into what it takes to think in the NoSQL way. Here, you will also learn how to make decisions based on reliability, performance, and complexity.

Data modeling for relational databases

A new application almost always starts with data modeling. In traditional data modeling for relational databases, this process is known as **data normalization**, which focuses on removing data redundancy and minimizing data dependency. The modeling formulates a series of tables, which are defined by its schema (rows and columns of the table).

Normalization

Why normalization? Data normalization helps to reduce dependency and redundancy of data, which makes it easier to update the data, while maintaining its consistency.

Normalization ensures that the update is done only once for an entity. Let's take a typical example to showcase how data normalization works:

ID	Name	Subject
1	John	Biology
2	Smith	Math
3	John	Math
4	Scott	Biology
5	Smith	Physics

In this example, the data in the Name field is repeating as one student can take multiple subjects. In normalization, it is required to have data that is tabular with each row-column intersection having one value. The redundancy of data can create inconsistencies in the data during updates, where there is a real possibility of the same data having different values. To make the preceding table normalized, we can consider adding another column for extra subjects, which looks something like this:

ID	Name	Subject_1	Subject_2
1	John	Math	Biology
2	Smith	Physics	Math
3	Scott	Biology	Null

The preceding structure creates its own problems. For instance, if you want to know all the students who are taking a Math class, you have to check two columns. The problem gets more complex if there is a student who is taking more than two subjects, which requires you to add a column to the table. Updating and deleting a record becomes more problematic.

In this scenario, to maintain consistency and to avoid redundancy, we have to create two tables. The first table will contain all the student information as follows:

Student_ID	Name
1	John
2	Smith
3	Scott

The second table will contain the information related to the subjects offered as follows:

Subject_ID	Subject_name
1	Biology
2	Math
3	Physics

Now, we have to create a map of uniquely identifiable IDs in the form of a table that shows which student is taking what subjects:

Student_ID	Subject_ID
1	1
1	2
2	2
2	3
3	1

In the preceding data model, we do not have to worry about data inconsistencies. This allows us to manipulate the data easily, and allows insertions and deletions of data without having to worry about artifacts. However, a problem arises when reading the data. If you want to know the name of the student who is taking Math, the SQL query will be as follows:

```
SELECT a.Name from STUDENTS a JOIN STU_SUB_MAP b ON a.student_id=b.
student_id JOIN SUBJECTS c ON c.Subject_id = b.Subject_id where
c.subject_name='Math'
```

The result of the query will look like the following table:

Name
John
Smith

Even though we have got the correct result from the database, the problem lies in the amount of work the database needs to do to get this result. It has to join three different tables, read the data, and display the results. The JOIN operation is a relatively expensive operation, which can be mitigated to some extent by using indexes. However, as the table size increases, the amount of time the database takes to compute also increases.

Though normalization gives us highly structured tables with the utmost consistency, sometimes we need to keep the data in a denormalized format. This is usually necessary in scenarios where performance takes precedence over structure. A denormalized structure is more beneficial if your application has much more reads than writes.

The NoSQL Way

The main advantage of NoSQL is that there is no concept of normalization. This is the reason why you get more performance from a NoSQL database when seen against a normalized SQL database. There is a trade-off in that you are sacrificing data consistency in the NoSQL database, but the benefits achieved in doing so are higher. Clearly, NoSQL databases are built with one central feature, which is performance. So in order to achieve performance, the data consistency and reliability are sacrificed at various levels.

Redis, as explained by the creator, is a key-value store. The data is always stored as key and value pairs. This means a lot of work needs to go into data modeling. There are no easy normalization steps like in SQL that instantly give us the tables. The data modeling needs to account for all the application data and closely binds to requirements of the application. In Redis, the key should be a string, but the value can be of many types, such as strings, lists, sets, hashes, and many more.

 Redis is not a SQL replacement. It works completely out of memory and is best suited for faster writes and random reads. In most cases, it cannot be used as the only data store in your application stack.

Revisiting the same student subject schema, there are many possibilities to store the same data in Redis. It also offers convenience to the user in terms of storing and retrieving the data. For example, we can use hashes on the student subject schema as follows:

```
HMSET JOHN subject1 Math subject2 Biology

HMSET SMITH subject1 Math subject2 Physics

HMSET SCOTT subject1 Biology
```

The above command uses the hashes data type in Redis and creates three hashes with the student name as key. If you want to get all the subjects taken by a student, you can use the following command:

```
HVALS SMITH
```

The preceding command will give the following output:

```
1) "Math"
2) "Physics"
```

A limitation with the previous structure is that it is difficult to update or delete a value from the student field due to the named field name for the hashes. We can achieve a similar result by using SET as follows:

```
SADD student:JOHN Math Biology
SADD student:SMITH Math Physics
SADD student:SCOTT Biology
```

If we would like to know the subjects taken by Scott, the command is simple: SMEMBERS SCOTT. In case we need to query for the subject, we can store the data as follows:

```
SADD subject:Math JOHN SMITH
SADD subject:Biology JOHN SCOTT
SADD subject:Physics SMITH
```

So, if we need to know the students taking Biology, we can use SMEMBERS Biology.

 If we are interested in knowing the students who are taking both Math and Biology, we can use SINTER Math Biology.

As we can see, data modeling on Redis entirely depends on what data we want to read back from it. However, in the case of an update or delete, we need to update both the subject set and student set.

Summary

The decision to use different data types and formats majorly depends on the access patterns of our application. We need to store denormalized data in case of reads and store partial normalized data in case of equal reads and writes to maintain consistency. The flexibility of Redis lets your application, if used correctly, take advantage of its powerful ultrafast data store. We will look into various data modeling examples in the upcoming chapters, where we will delve into more complex use case patterns. In the next chapter, we will look into how the transactions and locks work in Redis in comparison to the traditional SQL systems.

2
Transactions and Locks

Data consistency has always been one of the most paramount features in relational database systems. Consistency is maintained using transactions executing multiple atomic statements. The cardinal rule of a transaction is that either all statements succeed or all statements fail, while ensuring that the databases move from one consistent state to another. So, how can we maintain consistency in Redis where the concept of a transaction does not exist in the traditional sense?

In *Chapter 1*, *The SQL and NoSQL Way*, we discussed the difference between SQL and NoSQL. In this chapter, we will discuss transactions, how they are used in relational database systems, and how to achieve the same behavior in Redis in the absence of the transactions concept. Though we will take a deeper look into various data structures in Redis in the next chapter, this chapter gives an outline of a few basic data structures.

Transactions in SQL systems

In SQL databases, transactions are used to maintain **atomicity**, **consistency**, **isolation**, and **durability**, known as **ACID** for short. A typical example of a transaction is bank transfers. Debt from a bank account should successfully credit into another account. If the credit fails, the transaction should be rolled back to the initial state and the amount debited should be credited back.

These states are achieved using COMMIT on success and ROLLBACK on failure. Even though this works well in a single database system, the process becomes slow in a distributed database environment.

 In order to maintain consistency across multiple databases, statements are prepared and executed in all databases and only after getting a success message from all servers is the transaction completed. As the lock is maintained until all the servers commit, the application is slowed down in the process.

For example, in SQL systems, transactions are carried out as follows:

```
BEGIN TRANSACTION;
DELETE FROM tbl_students WHERE user_id='3';
DELETE FROM tbl_student_subjects WHERE user_id='3';
COMMIT;
```

In the preceding scenario, if there is an error in the second query, the user is not deleted from the `tbl_students` table. Effectively, no rows are deleted. In most SQL systems, we can achieve the same behavior through cascading constraints. By using a constraint, we execute the same statement as follows:

```
DELETE FROM tbl_students WHERE id='3';
```

In this scenario, the query is translated to a previous query by the SQL engine. This makes sure we always delete the information related to a student when we delete the student to maintain consistency.

Maintaining data consistency in Redis

A programmer who is new to Redis can translate the previous schema into the following Redis data structure:

- Hashes for students:

  ```
  HMSET Stud:1 Name John ID 1
  HMSET Stud:2 Name Smith ID 2
  HMSET Stud:3 Name Scott ID 3
  ```

- Hashes for subjects:

  ```
  HMSET Sub:1 Name Math Room_No 201
  HMSET Sub:2 Name Physics Room_No 2106
  HMSET Sub:3 Name Biology Room_No 5105
  ```

- Simple SET for students to subjects mapping:

  ```
  SADD Map_Stud_1 Sub_1 Sub_3
  SADD Map_Stud_2 Sub_1 Sub_2
  ```

So, the hashes (Stud:*) has the information about students, hashes (Sub:*) has the information about Subjects, and the string has the information about the subjects enrolled by the students.

Chapter 2

If you have not realized it yet, the major problem here is that to get the number of students who have taken a particular subject, we need to iterate through all the sets. Otherwise, we need to create another set with the subject as key and students as values. What is very obvious in the relational database is not as obvious in Redis as everything needs to be designed based on how we want to access the data.

Now, if you want to delete a student from our database, you can do this as follows:

```
DEL Stud_:1
```

By doing so, there is a possibility of having stale data in our mapping sets for the student Stud:1 as it is not deleted. In order to be consistent, you need to delete the data from its present occurrences, which includes iterating through all the subjects sets to remove the student. Considering this situation, we can optimize by embedding the subjects as part of students hashes as follows:

```
HMSET Stud:1 Name John ID 1 Subject "Sub:1,Sub:3"
HMSET Stud:2 Name Smith ID 2 Subject "Sub:1,Sub:2"
```

Now, in order to delete a user, we can just use DEL Stud:1, which will delete all the information about a student along with the subjects a student is enrolled in. However, on the negative side, updating a student is going to be difficult as we need to parse the comma-separated values to get individual subjects.

Transactions in Redis

Transactions in Redis are just a way of supporting execution of a series of commands atomically. All the commands issued by the client will be queued in the server until they are executed or discarded. The MULTI, EXEC, DISCARD, and WATCH commands are the foundation of transactions in Redis. Now, we want to delete the student from hash and also make sure the mapping set is deleted. We can use transactions as follows:

```
MULTI
DEL Stud:1
DEL Map_Stud_1
EXEC
```

There is no rollback in Redis. Even if the second DEL statement fails, the Stud:1 key will be deleted. The philosophy behind lack of rollback is that in Redis, a command can fail only due to syntax errors or programming errors, such as unsupported operations on different data types. So, it does not make sense to support rollback for programming errors, which will anyway become a bug in the application.

The WATCH command is used to provide a **check-and-set** (**CAS**) behavior to Redis transactions. The WATCH command is used to make sure the transaction is executed only when other clients modify none of the watched keys. For example, let's say we want to remove the top player from a real-time leaderboard. We have to make sure the top player does not change while we are calculating the leader. The following set of commands will explain how the WATCH command works:

```
WATCH leaderboard element = ZREVRANGEBYSCORE leaderboard +inf -inf
WITHSCORES
MULTI
ZREM leaderboard element
EXEC
```

If the leaderboard gets updated before we remove the item from the sorted set, the EXEC command is never executed. We will learn more use cases of transactions in later chapters.

Summary

In Redis, the Watch command provides the necessary lock mechanism and the multi/exec/discard commands allow us to execute commands atomically. The flexibility of locking and transaction gives us a very powerful system when we understand how Redis works. In the next chapter, we will discuss various data types available in Redis, which will be useful to build some complex systems in a later part of the book.

3
Data Types in Redis

In *Chapter 2, Transactions and Locks*, we learned about the transactions and locks in Redis. However, in order to leverage the full potential of Redis, one needs to understand the basic data types built into it. The data types are very powerful and provide full atomic operations for data manipulation.

These data types are flexible and can be used or exploited in a lot of ways. In order to design solutions using Redis, we need to understand what each data type means, how to use them, when to use a data type, and more importantly, when not to use a data type.

In this chapter, we will focus on the following topics:

- Understanding the different data types in Redis
- When to use each data type
- Key expiry in Redis
- Key namespace and naming conventions

Understanding the different data types in Redis

Strings, lists, hashes, sets, and sorted sets are the basic data types in Redis. Each type has its strengths and should be used appropriately to take complete advantage of these strengths. In this section, we will discuss each type briefly.

 To view all the available commands and data types in Redis, visit http://redis.io/commands.

Strings

Strings are the most basic data type in Redis. This basic type is binary safe and is used to create more complex data types such as lists and sets. A string value can hold up to 512 MB of data. Being the most basic type, it can be used to hold anything such as a binary stream of images, data in JSON format, generated HTML cached for faster delivery, and many other use cases.

From Redis 2.6.12, we can even set expiry information in seconds or milliseconds as part of the SET command. Prior to 2.6.12, we can set expiry information through the SETEX command with seconds' precision.

```
SET mykey myvalue EX 5
GET mykey
```

The preceding commands will create a key with the name mykey and set it to a value of myvalue. Also, the expiry is set to five seconds. After five seconds, the key will be expired. To understand how the expiry works and the accuracy of expiry in Redis, visit http://redis.io/commands/expire.

Lists

In Redis, lists are lists of binary-safe strings arranged based on the order of insertion. This ensures that the data can be accessed in the same order in which it was inserted. Internally, lists are implemented using a basic linked list, which has both pros and cons.

The advantage is that adding an element in the head or tail of the list takes the same time. For example, adding an item to a list with 10 items or 10,000 items takes an equal amount of time, but the main disadvantage is that accessing an element in the middle of the list takes longer than accessing elements near the extremes. This makes it ideal to build any data structure where we want to work only with extremes (near the head or tail).

 The lookup operation is O(N), where N is the index of the element.

Lists are ideal for modeling queues or stacks for event logging. Possible in-built operations make it easy to manipulate the list data.

Sets

Sets are a set of binary-safe strings that are a collection of *unique unsorted elements*. Sets cannot hold duplicate members. You should consider using sets when you have a collection of items and you need to add, delete, or verify the existence of members in a very efficient and fast manner. Another desired behavior is no duplication, and also support for peek and pop of elements (using the SRANDMEMBER and SPOP commands). Sets can store up to 232-1 elements.

> Redis sets provide a constant time *O(1)* for all the mentioned operations, irrespective of the number of items you have in the set.

Sets support complex operations under the fold such as UNION and INTERSECTION between different sets. Sets are one of the most important data types that make complex data types possible.

Sets should be used when we have a list of items and we want to check whether an item exists in the list in an efficient manner. It is also good for random lookups and to maintain indexes. If we want to create indexes or inverted indexes to perform a search, sets are ideal for this type of problem.

Sorted sets

Consider sorted sets as improved sets. While sets are unordered, sorted sets, as the name suggests, are sorted based on associative scores; an additional operation to the query based on score ranges. This is the most advanced and complex data type in Redis so far. The associated scores are used to sort the set from the smallest to the greatest score. We can add, delete, or update elements in a sorted set quickly because elements are inserted in an order rather than ordered afterwards. To really understand the functionality of sorted sets, we will look into the following example of building a priority queue:

```
ZADD p_queue 100 "task1"
ZADD p_queue 400 "task2"
ZADD p_queue 20 "task3"
ZRANGE p_queue 0 -1
```

The result will be as follows:

```
1) "task3"
2) "task1"
3) "task2"
```

If we want to reverse the order from maximum to minimum score, use the following command:

```
zrevrange p_queue 0 -1
```

If another task needs to be added, use the following command:

```
ZADD p_queue 40 "task4"
```

Now, the `zrevrange p_queue 0 -1` command results in the following output:

```
1)  "task2"

2)  "task1"

3)  "task4"

4)  "task3"
```

 Every time we add an element, the server performs an *O(log(N))* operation.

Due to the ordered behavior and optimization, sorted sets are best suited to maintain leaderboards, timestamp data ranges, or to implement auto-completion with Redis. They make good priority queues and can be used to implement weighted random selections.

Hashes

Hashes are perfect to represent objects as a map between string fields and string values. Hashes are equivalent to a hash table or a hash map in Java. If we need to store some data related to an object and do not want to perform encoding (in JSON or XML, for example), hashes are the ideal solution. Hashes can be used to represent linked data structures using references.

 Complex data structures can be created using hashes by creating a hash with a reference to lists and sets.

Hashes can be simple, as shown in the following command lines:

```
HMSET id:1765 name "Hari Seldon" profession "Mathematician"

HSET id:1765 profession "PyschoHistorian"

HGETALL id:1765
```

The difference between the HMSET and HSET command is while HSET can add a value to a single hash field, HMSET can set multiple hash fields with values in the same command.

Hashes are perfect to store objects with fields and values and to represent linked data structures such as sets through reference.

HyperLogLog

HyperLogLog is a probabilistic data structure used to count unique items. For example, we want to know the number of unique search terms searched in our site or the number of unique products that are viewed by the visitors; we need to store the terms or IDs in a list and add to the list after checking whether the item already exists. To achieve this, the amount of memory required is proportional to the number of items in the list we are counting. HyperLogLog is an approximation algorithm that sacrifices the precision for memory. In the case of Redis implementation, the standard error is less than 1 percent and the memory used is far less.

 To find out more about HyperLogLog implementation in Redis, check out http://antirez.com/news/75.

PFADD is the command used to add the items, whereas PFCOUNT is used to retrieve the approximate count of unique items, as shown in the following example:

```
(integer) 1
PFADD terms hello hi howdy
PFCOUNT terms
(integer) 3
```

Key expiration

The EXPIRE command in Redis is used to set time-to-live for keys. The keys with expiry set are volatile. After the timeout has expired, the key will automatically be deleted. The timeout can also be cleared, turning the key back into a persistent key using the PERSIST command. It is important to know the basics of autoexpiry of keys for future chapters. The concept of expiry mechanisms is vast and is not covered as part of this book.

 To find out more about expiry mechanisms and how they work in Redis, visit http://redis.io/commands/expire.

Autoexpiry makes Redis ideal to store volatile information such as session information or for caching contents for a specific time.

Summary

All these data types make Redis unique and make it stand out from other NoSQL solutions. These basic types can be used to create more complex data structures by embedding or referencing the key names from other values. For example, we can create a sorted set, which contains the key name of hashes as reference. When designing the application using Redis, more than relational systems, we need to make more effort in designing the schema. In the next chapter, we will see how to use some of these data types to build a caching server using Redis.

4
Redis as a Caching Server

In *Chapter 3, Data Types in Redis*, we learned about the data types in Redis. In this chapter, we will see how the data types can be used to create different systems. The first use case of Redis that we will explore is in cache management. In today's computing environment, caching is everywhere. It is the easiest way to scale an application, and is usually achieved by computing once and delivering the same item for a limited time by storing it in a temporary medium. The request for the data can be delivered from the cache rather than undertaking a compute action every time.

With less than 10 milliseconds access time for a record during typical benchmarking and complex data structure support, Redis is one of the best data stores when it comes to caching. In this chapter, we will focus on the following areas in building a caching server:

- Simple caching server
- Memory optimization technique to save memory
- Sharding of cache data across multiple Redis instances

What is caching

Caching is used to store application data, which is expensive to generate during runtime. Therefore, instead of generating data every time a user requests for it, we compute it once and deliver the cached data every time until the cache data is invalidated. This usually improves response time and reduces the need for processing power drastically. The invalidation could be time dependent or dependent on data change. Caching in itself is a huge topic and cannot be explained in a lot of detail in this book. However, we will be learning about how Redis can be used effectively to cache data in later sections.

For the sake of simplicity, consider we have a web page, which shows a set of 30 products with a distinct dataset for each title, image, and price. The ordering of the products as well as the selection is based on the popularity and diversity logic of the application. We know for a fact that the price of the product does not change for six hours and that the title and image data of the product is always consistent and will never change. So, instead of generating the page every time a user visits, we can cache the complete page for six hours and deliver the same content to every user without any extra computation. This will improve the response time and in turn increase user engagement. This is where Redis comes into play.

The solution overview

Though it is very easy to implement a caching server by using the SET and GET operations, the solution provided here takes advantage of the advanced memory optimization feature in Redis. We will look into a simple solution and then dive into the optimization problem to reduce memory usage.

Simple SET and GET cache servers

If the data to be cached is small and in the range of a few megabytes, we can use a single server with a single Redis instance. In this case, the SET and GET commands are sufficient. For instance, the web page to cache takes the URI as a parameter and generates the page. Then, we store the page contents as a value to a unique key. In this case, instead of storing URI as the key, we can use the hash of URI. Refer to the following PHP code sample in which we consider $redis to be the Predis object:

```
$redis = new Predis\Client([
   'scheme' => 'tcp',
   'host'   => '127.0.0.1',
   'port'   => 6379,
]);

$uri = $_SERVER['REQUEST_URI'];
if ($redis->exists(md5($uri))) {
   $contents = $redis->get(md5($uri));
   echo $contents;
   exit();
}
/* Operations to generate the page and assign the output to a variable
$contents */

$redis->set(md5($uri), $contents);
```

When a user visits the same URL now, the cache will be delivered directly from Redis. If we are interested in the implicit expiry of the cache after x seconds of time, we can take advantage of expiry operations in Redis by adding the following command after the SET operation:

```
$redis->expire(md5($uri), 6*60*60) //6 Hours validity
```

This is the simplest cache system that can be implemented using Redis with less than 10 lines of code. However, in this case, we will have 100K key-value pairs if we want to cache 100K pages. If we want to store the data efficiently, we need to take advantage of special encoding of small aggregate data types in Redis. We will see how to do that next.

In Redis, there is a memory optimization technique implemented that gives you the ability to reduce the usage of RAM with a trade-off occurring with the CPU processing time if the size of the data structure is small. The amount of optimization can be controlled easily by altering the following variables in the Redis configuration file:

- hash-max-ziplist-entries 256
- hash-max-ziplist-value 512

 To find out more about memory optimization techniques, visit http://redis.io/topics/memory-optimization.

Once the number of entries or values exceeds the configured number, Redis converts the data back to normal encoding, which is transparent to the user and fast for smaller datasets. Our aim is to keep the size below the configured values so that our caching server can take full advantage of this feature. Instead of using SET and GET, we will use the hashes data type now. Each value in a hash will be the cached data. In this example, let's say we want to cache user pages. Assume we have 10,000 users on our website and each user has a dedicated page in which they can view their wish list and personalized data with a constraint being that the data does not change for two hours.

 In case we need to continue using the URL as key, we can convert the URL into an integer variable using MD5 or any hashing functions with less collision in order to shard the data using the same logic.

In order to use special encoding, we need to store these 10,000 user pages into 20 hashes each with 512 entries for each user (hash-max-ziplist-value 512).

The previous code snippet will now be:

```
$userId = $_GET['userid'];
$key = "USER:" . floor($userId / 512);
```

```
$field = $userId % 512;

if ($redis->hexists($key, $field) {
  $contents = $redis->hget($key, $field);
  echo $contents;
  exit();
}
/* Operations to generate the page and assign the output to a variable
$contents */

$redis->hset($key, $field, $contents);
```

In the preceding instance, we have sharded user data into various hashes based on their user ID. With the current configuration, we can support up to 131072 users (256 X 512) and take advantage of special encoding for all users. If you need to add more users, all you have to do is update the variables: `hash-max-ziplist-entries` and `hash-max-ziplist-value`, or use multiple Redis instances in the same server and perform sharding across the instance.

> This same logic can be used not only to store HTML, but also JSON, XML, or any other data structure that we are interested in caching.

In the case of most consumer websites such as Instagram, Craigslist, and others, the data to be cached or stored is too huge and cannot be accommodated in a single Redis instance or even on the same server. In such cases, we may need to store data across multiple servers. Let's discuss how such an operation can be performed.

For this case, assume we have around a million users and we want to cache the data across four different Redis instances, each consisting of 262144 users. So, we will go ahead and update the `redis.conf` file with updated configuration values as follows:

```
hash-max-ziplist-entries 512

hash-max-ziplist-value 512
```

Since we want to use multiple servers, we need to maintain our own array of Redis instances and use similar functions to find the Redis instance to store the key name and field name.

> If we just want to handle more cache data, we can add more servers to the system as we are using consistent hashing. The same is not true for Redis as it is just a data store.

In the case of PHP, `Predis` supports consistent hashing implicitly. You can simply achieve the same behavior by defining multiple instances. Predis will take the responsibility of choosing the Redis instance for you based on the hashing function implemented. All the major languages have a library, which supports client-side sharding. The following code snippet lets you shard the data across multiple Redis servers automatically when using the `Predis` library:

```
$redis = new Predis\Client([
    'tcp://127.0.0.1:6379?alias=first-node',
    'tcp://127.0.0.1:6381?alias=second-node',
    'tcp://10.232.55.50:6379?alias=third-node',
    'tcp://10.232.55.51:6379?alias=fourth-node',
]);
```

In the case of other languages, check the library documentation. If not supported, you need to maintain an array of Redis instances to achieve client-side sharding.

Summary

In this chapter, we discussed how to use Redis for implementing a simple caching server. The caching server can be a single instance or multiple instances on the same server node or multiple instances across multiple servers. Now that we have seen the most basic functions of Redis, in the next chapter we shall discuss more complex use cases that involve more complex Redis functionalities and data structures in the e-commerce industry.

5
Redis in an E-commerce Inventory System

Our next venture in Redis is to understand how to leverage Redis for the retail industry, focusing mainly on e-commerce websites. The benefits offered by Redis can be utilized mainly in two areas: product catalog management and inventory management systems. A product catalog is the main component of any e-commerce application, while managing inventory is just as vital. As such, we will see how we can use Redis to maintain an efficient catalog and also perform a real-time search over the product inventory in the first use case.

In the second use case, we will see how to use Redis to manage an inventory and simplify the checkout process.

A product catalog

Every e-commerce application starts with a product catalog. An efficient product catalog should be able to store huge lists of products, each with their own different attributes. The schemaless design of Redis comes in handy in this regard as it allows you to create a flexible design structure that stores all the necessary values in hashes.

Consider the following case in which we want to store information about a set of books in our catalog. The information in the following table needs to be stored as part of our catalog information:

Attributes	Item 1	Item 2
Title	Instance Redis Persistence	Instant Redis optimisation How-To
Author	Matt Palmer	Arun Chinnachamy
ISBN	9781783280216	9781782164807
Language	English	English
Release date	Dec 2013	May 2013
Price	$11	$12
URL	http://www.packtpub.com/redis-persistence/book	http://www.packtpub.com/redis-optimization-how-to/book
Available Format	e-Book	e-Book & Paperback

We can store this information in hashes with all of the attributes as a field:

```
HMSET catalog:book:9781783280216 title "Instant Redis Persistence
[Instant]" author "Matt Palmer" language "English" release-date "December
2013" price "11" URL "http://www.packtpub.com/redis-persistence/book"
available_format "Ebook"
```

```
HMSET catalog:book:9781782164807 title "Instant Redis Optimization How-to
[Instant]" author "Arun Chinnachamy" language "English" release-date "May
2013" price "12" URL "http://www.packtpub.com/redis-optimization-how-to/
book" available_format "Ebook, Paperback"
```

For further operations, we can come up with a different schema design based on our use case. Let's consider a catalog search as the first use case.

The catalog search

Let's say we want to search the entire catalog and provide relevant results with the product information. We want to search only on the title of the product. To achieve this, we can iterate through all the hashes and search the title. However, what is the fun in doing that? Let's see how to perform the same search by making our own data structure, which allows us to be more efficient.

Either sorted sets or hashes can be used for this operation. We can start by populating another hash with the title as the field and the value of the field as the product ID (which is the ISBN number in our case):

```
HMSET catalog:search "Instant Redis Persistence [Instant]"
"9781783280216" "Instant Redis Optimization How-to [Instant]"
"9781782164807"
```

In an event where we want to search using the author name, we can easily modify the hashes by adding these values as fields and setting new product ID values. Now to search using the author name, use the HSCAN operation, which was introduced in Redis 2.8.0, as follows:

```
HSCAN catalog:search 0 MATCH *Instant* COUNT 20
```

 To find out more about how HSCAN works, check out http://redis.io/commands/hscan.

The result will contain all matched titles along with the ISBN numbers of the books. To display the results, we can do another *O(1)* operation to retrieve all the product details from the catalog:book hashes.

To paginate the results and retrieve the next set of results, we need to set the cursor to the value returned by the last HSCAN command. We need to continue executing HSCAN till the cursor value returned by Redis is zero. In case the number of values returned by Redis is zero but the cursor value is not zero, we need to execute the HSCAN command again to fetch the result. Assuming the last returned cursor by Redis is 32, the command to fetch the next set of result is as follows:

```
HSCAN catalog:search 32 MATCH *instant* COUNT 20
```

According to the Redis official website, Redis can iterate 1 million keys in 40 milliseconds. So for a medium-sized catalog size with around 100K products, the solution will provide results in less than 100 milliseconds. The key to achieve this is to index everything. Then, in the search hashes, we can include all the fields we want to be searchable mapped to the same value (ISBN).

 If you are planning to perform a lot of search text queries, look into search index engines such as Apache SOLR or Elastic Search.

Inventory management

Inventory management is a critical part of any e-commerce system. It is a basic expectation from all users that any online retail website will not let you order items unless they are available. This part of the book covers a basic overview about the inventory system data model in Redis.

Let's begin by assuming that a user's shopping cart shows the following information: item title, order quantity, and order price. Every user will have their own cart and should be able to add any number of items into their carts. For the sake of simplicity, we will not update the inventory on adding to cart and we will not let the user checkout unless we have the item in stock.

The solution overview

Like we discussed earlier, we will start by storing the item in hashes as follows:

```
HMSET catalog:item:1 title "Awesome Product 1" price 10 available_
quantity 4
```

```
HMSET catalog:item:2 title "Awesome Product 2" price 14 available_
quantity 0
```

```
HMSET catalog:item:3 title "Awesome Product 3" price 12 available_
quantity 2
```

```
HMSET catalog:item:4 title "Awesome Product 4" price 29 available_
quantity 16
```

Let's now look at how to store the user cart data. Assume we have a user with the following data:

```
HMSET user:1000:cart:1 "catalog:item:1" 1 "catalog:item:4" 2
```

This cart means the user with an ID 1000 has one quantity of item 1 and two quantities of item 4. In this case, we are using a reference to the original product data to avoid inconsistency between the cart and the product catalog. Furthermore, it is best that we avoid storing any pricing data in the cart data to avoid inconsistency in pricing between the catalog and the cart. By doing this, we ensure that the latest price is the one that is seen by the user at all times. Also, if there is a change in the price between the time the item is added to the cart and the time a user checks out, we ensure that the user will see the updated price rather than the old price.

To add an item into a user cart, we need to perform a few checks, which are outlined as follows:

1. Make sure the item is in stock.
2. Add the item into the user's cart.
3. On error or change of quantity, rollback the available quantity.

Now, consider a scenario wherein a user with ID 2000 wants to add item 3 into his cart. Let's see what the sample code looks like in PHP:

```
$product_key = 'catalog:item:3';
$user_key = 'user:2000:cart:9';
$options = array('cad'=>true , 'watch'=>$product_key, 'retry'=>3);
$redis->transaction($options, function ($tx) use ($product_key, $user_
key, $redis) {
  $available_quantity = $redis->hget($product_key,
    "available_quantity);
  if($available_quantity >= $order_quantity) {
    $redis->hset($user_key, $product_key, $order_quantity); }
  else {
    // Throw error saying that the item is not in stock.
  }
});
```

In this piece of code, we have used a transaction along with CAS operations using MULTI/EXEC. In doing so, we can track the product catalog to prevent simultaneous changes to the available quantity. Transactions in Redis do not work the same way they do in relations database systems, as Redis does not support transaction rollback. If an error occurs during a transaction, all the operations performed before that statement are committed and cannot be rolled back automatically. This is due to the fact that Redis is designed to be faster and does not necessarily include the functionality that is needed for error handling. An error during the transaction can occur due to any number of factors that include syntax errors or operations on the wrong data type.

To find out more about WATCH and transactions in Redis, visit http://redis.io/topics/transactions.

To update the order quantity, we can use the same hset function, which overrides the existing value. This can be used in an event where we want to let the items in the cart expire after a certain time. We can easily facilitate this functionality by using the expiry operation in Redis. The following query makes sure the cart is deleted after a day:

```
$redis->expiry($user_key, 24*60*60);
```

During checkout, we need to perform the following operations for each product in the cart:

1. Make sure we have sufficient quantity of items in stock.

2. Decrement from the product inventory.

3. Update the status of the cart and remove expiry, if any.

Here's the code snippet to perform the aforementioned operations:

```
$product_key = 'catalog:item:3';
$user_key = 'user:2000:cart:9';
$options = array('cad'=>true , 'watch'=>$product_key, 'retry'=>3);

$redis->transaction($options, function ($tx) use ($product_key, $user_
key, $redis) {
  $available_quantity = $redis->hget($product_key, "available_
quantity);

  if($available_quantity >= $order_quantity) {
    $redis->hincrby($product_key, 'available_quantity',
      ($order_quantity * -1));
    $redis->hset($user_key, 'Status:COMPLETE', time());
    $redis->expiry($user_key, '-1');
  } else {
  // throw error saying the item is not in stock.
  }
});
```

On successful checkout, we set another field as Status:COMPLETE during the time of checkout. In case we want to bring all of the items in the cart into a COMPLETE status, we can use the HSCAN operation. Another option would be to copy the information to another hashes query for easier access to the checked-out cart.

Make sure to use transactions to avoid inconsistency between the catalog and cart.

 If the data is huge and cannot fit into a single instance, consider sharding the data across multiple instances using a consistent hashing logic.

Summary

In this chapter, we have seen how to use hashes to store an e-commerce catalog and perform search over data. We have also understood how to use transactions along with CAS in Redis for the inventory management system. In the next chapter, we will see how to perform autosuggest and facet searching with Redis, which is commonly used in almost all e-commerce online portals.

6
Redis in Autosuggest

In *Chapter 5*, *Redis in an E-commerce Inventory System*, we saw how to use Redis in an e-commerce catalog for product and inventory management. We also saw how to perform a catalog search. While Redis is not the best solution for searching a catalog, it is ideal when it comes to implementing an autosuggest and basic facet search.

In this chapter, we are going to see how to use Redis to build a basic autocomplete or autosuggest server. Also, we will see how to build a faceting engine using Redis. To build such a system, we will use sorted sets and operations involving ranges and intersections. To summarize, we will focus on the following topics in this chapter:

- Autocompletion for words
- Multiword autosuggestion using a sorted set
- Faceted search using sets and operations such as union and intersection

Autosuggest systems

These days autosuggest is seen in virtually all e-commerce stores in addition to a host of others. Almost all websites are utilizing this functionality in one way or another from a basic website search to programming IDEs. The ease of use afforded by autosuggest has led every major website from Google and Amazon to Wikipedia to use this feature to make it easier for users to navigate to where they want to go. The primary metric for any autosuggest system is how fast we can respond with suggestions to a user's query. Usability research studies have found that the response time should be under a second to ensure that a user's attention and flow of thought are preserved. Redis is ideally suited for this task as it is one of the fastest data stores in the market right now.

Let's see how to design such a structure and use Redis to build an autosuggest engine. We can tweak Redis to suit individual use case scenarios, ranging from the simple to the complex. For instance, if we want only to autocomplete a word, we can enable this functionality by using a sorted set. Let's see how to perform single word completion and then we will move on to more complex scenarios, such as phrase completion.

Word completion in Redis

In this section, we want to provide a simple word completion feature through Redis. We will use a sorted set for this exercise. The reason behind using a sorted set is that it always guarantees $O(\log(N))$ operations. While it is commonly known that in a sorted set, elements are arranged based on the score, what is not widely acknowledged is that elements with the same scores are arranged lexicographically. This is going to form the basis for our word completion feature. Let's look at a scenario in which we have the words to autocomplete: jack, smith, scott, jacob, and jackeline.

In order to complete a word, we need to use n-gram. Every word needs to be written as a contiguous sequence.

 n-gram is a contiguous sequence of *n* items from a given sequence of text or speech. To find out more, check http://en.wikipedia.org/wiki/N-gram.

For example, n-gram of jack is as follows:

j

ja

jac

jack$

In order to signify the completed word, we can use a delimiter such as * or $. To add the word into a sorted set, we will be using ZADD in the following way:

```
> zadd autocomplete 0 j
> zadd autocomplete 0 ja
> zadd autocomplete 0 jac
> zadd autocomplete 0 jack$
```

Likewise, we need to add all the words we want to index for autocompletion. Once we are done, our sorted set will look as follows:

```
> zrange autocomplete 0 -1
1)  "j"
2)  "ja"
3)  "jac"
4)  "jack$"
5)  "jacke"
6)  "jackel"
7)  "jackeli"
8)  "jackelin"
9)  "jackeline$"
10) "jaco"
11) "jacob$"
12) "s"
13) "sc"
14) "sco"
15) "scot"
16) "scott$"
17) "sm"
18) "smi"
19) "smit"
20) "smith$"
```

Now, we will use ZRANK and ZRANGE operations over the sorted set to achieve our desired functionality. To autocomplete for ja, we have to execute the following commands:

```
> zrank autocomplete jac
2
zrange autocomplete 3 50
1)  "jack$"
2)  "jacke"
3)  "jackel"
4)  "jackeli"
5)  "jackelin"
```

```
 6) "jackeline$"
 7) "jaco"
 8) "jacob$"
 9) "s"
10) "sc"
11) "sco"
12) "scot"
13) "scott$"
14) "sm"
15) "smi"
16) "smit"
17) "smith$"
```

Another example on completing `smi` is as follows:

```
zrank autocomplete smi
17
zrange autocomplete 18 50
1) "smit"
2) "smith$"
```

Now, in our program, we have to do the following tasks:

1. Iterate through the results set.
2. Check if the word starts with the query and only use the words with $ as the last character.

Though it looks like a lot of operations are performed, both ZRANGE and ZRANK are $O(log(N))$ operations. Therefore, there should be virtually no problem in handling a huge list of words. When it comes to memory usage, we will have $n+1$ elements for every word, where n is the number of characters in the word. For M words, we will have $M(avg(n) + 1)$ records where $avg(n)$ is the average characters in a word. The more the collision of characters in our universe, the less the memory usage.

In order to conserve memory, we can use the EXPIRE command to expire unused long tail autocomplete terms.

Multiword phrase completion

In the previous section, we have seen how to use the autocomplete for a single word. However, in most real world scenarios, we will have to deal with multiword phrases. This is much more difficult to achieve as there are a few inherent challenges involved:

- Suggesting a phrase for all matching words. For instance, the same manufacturer has a lot of models available. We have to ensure that we list all models if a user decides to search for a manufacturer by name.

- Order the results based on overall popularity and relevance of the match instead of ordering lexicographically. The following screenshot shows the typical autosuggest box, which you find in popular e-commerce portals. This feature improves the user experience and also reduces the spell errors:

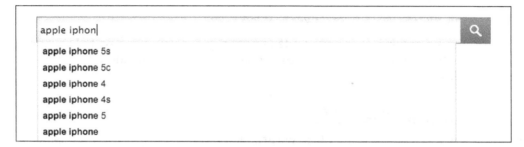

For this case, we will use a sorted set along with hashes. We will use a sorted set to store the n-gram of the indexed data followed by getting the complete title from hashes. Instead of storing the n-grams into the same sorted set, we will store them in different sorted sets.

Let's look at the following scenario in which we have model names of mobile phones along with their popularity:

Model names	Popularity
Samsung Galaxy Note 3	8
Samsung Galaxy Nexus	7
Apple iPhone 5S	9
Apple iPhone 5C	6

For this set, we will create multiple sorted sets. Let's take Apple iPhone 5S:

```
ZADD a 9 apple_iphone_5s
ZADD ap 9 apple_iphone_5s
ZADD app 9 apple_iphone_5s
ZADD apple 9 apple_iphone_5s
ZADD i 9 apple_iphone_5s
ZADD ip 9 apple_iphone_5s
ZADD iph 9 apple_iphone_5s
ZADD ipho 9 apple_iphone_5s
ZADD iphon 9 apple_iphone_5s
ZADD iphone 9 apple_iphone_5s
ZADD 5 9 apple_iphone_5s
ZADD 5s 9 apple_iphone_5s
HSET titles apple_iphone_5s "Apple iPhone 5S"
```

In the preceding scenario, we have added every n-gram value as a sorted set and created a hash that holds the original title. Likewise, we have to add all the titles into our index.

Searching in the index

Now that we have indexed the titles, we are ready to perform a search. Consider a situation where a user is querying with the term apple. We want to show the user the five best suggestions based on the popularity of the product. Here's how we can achieve this:

```
> zrevrange apple 0 4 withscores
1) "apple_iphone_5s"
2) 9.0
3) "apple_iphone_5c"
4) 6.0
```

As the elements inside the sorted set are ordered by the element score, we get the matches ordered by the popularity which we inserted. To get the original title, type the following command:

```
> hmget titles apple_iphone_5s
1) "Apple iPhone 5S"
```

In the preceding scenario case, the query was a single word. Now imagine if the user has multiple words such as Samsung nex, and we have to suggest the autocomplete as Samsung Galaxy Nexus. To achieve this, we will use ZINTERSTORE as follows:

```
> zinterstore samsung_nex 2 samsung nex aggregate max
```

ZINTERSTORE destination numkeys key [key ...] [WEIGHTS weight [weight ...]] [AGGREGATE SUM|MIN|MAX]

This computes the intersection of sorted sets given by the specified keys and stores the result in a destination. It is mandatory to provide the number of input keys before passing the input keys and other (optional) arguments. For more information about ZINTERSTORE, visit http://redis.io/commands/ZINTERSTORE.

The previous command, which is `zinterstore samsung_nex 2 samsung nex aggregate max`, will compute the intersection of two sorted sets, `samsung` and `nex`, and stores it in another sorted set, `samsung_nex`. To see the result, type the following commands:

```
> zrevrange samsung_nex 0 4 withscores
1) samsung_galaxy_nexus
2) 7
> hmget titles samsung_galaxy_nexus
1) Samsung Galaxy Nexus
```

If you want to cache the result for multiword queries and remove it automatically, use an EXPIRE command and set expiry for temporary keys.

The faceted search

The faceted search or faceted browsing is used for accessing information based on the classification system. It is used in almost all e-commerce stores and makes it easier for users to find products. It works by narrowing the search results through structured data and price ranges.

In this part, we will see how Redis can be used for faceted search. Let's take an example in which we want to create a facet search on mobile phones based on manufacturer, operating system, and SIM type.

We will be using sets to perform the facet search. As our access pattern is to showcase the properties of the product, we have to create a reverse index on properties and store individual product details in a hash.

```
HMSET phone:1 title "Apple iPhone 5S"
SADD OS:iOS phone:1
```

```
SADD Manufacturer:Apple phone:1
SADD SIM:Single phone:1

HMSET phone:2 title "Samsung Galaxy S5"
SADD OS:Android phone:2
SADD Manufacturer:Samsung phone:2
SADD SIM:Single phone:2

HMSET phone:3 title "Samsung Galaxy Grand 2"
SADD OS:Android phone:3
SADD Manufacturer:Samsung phone:3
SADD SIM:Dual phone:3

HMSET phone:4 title "Samsung Wave 3"
SADD OS:Bada phone:4
SADD Manufacturer:Samsung phone:4
SADD SIM:Single phone:4
```

Now, let's say that the user wants to see all the phones manufactured by Samsung. It will be a simple lookup in Redis to get all the phones by using set Manufacturer:Samsung as follows:

```
> SMEMBERS Manufacturer:Samsung
1) "phone:2"
2) "phone:3"
3) "phone:4"
```

We can perform HMGET on each ID to get the required information about the phones. Now that we have all mobiles manufactured by Samsung, let's look at how to further categorize the list and only show Samsung devices that run on Google's Android operating system. Now, we need to intersect between the two sorted sets as follows:

```
> SINTER Manufacturer:Samsung OS:Android
1) "phone:2"
2) "phone:3"
```

To further refine the search, we can add more filters. For instance, to retrieve a list of Android dual-SIM mobiles manufactured by Samsung, we can use the following command:

```
> SINTER Manufacturer:Samsung OS:Android SIM:Dual
1) "phone:3"
```

Voila! Now we have a data store which we can use to perform a faceted search. To know the results for any search, it will take a maximum $O(N*M)$ number of iterations, where N is the cardinality of the smallest set and M is the number of sets. There is another $O(1)$ lookup for getting product information from hashes.

 If you want to perform a search along with a faceted search or want to perform complex faceting, consider using SOLR (https://lucene.apache.org/solr/).

Summary

In this chapter, we have seen how to perform autosuggest and faceted searches using Redis. We have also understood how sorted sets and sets work. In the upcoming chapters, we will be discussing more complex usage of sorted sets in which we will see how to maintain priority and leverage sorted sets for building and maintaining leaderboards. In the next chapter, we will focus on how Redis can be used to perform real-time analysis of data and also how it can be used in analytics.

Redis in Real-time Analysis

In this chapter, we will explore how to deploy Redis in the domain of operational intelligence, in which we convert huge chunks of data into actionable business intelligence. In this chapter, we will also see how and why Redis is ideal as a primary session management data store so that the session data can be easily used for data analysis.

Redis in an analytics system

To perform any operations in analytics systems, one should perform the following steps:

1. Capture the data.
2. Process the information.
3. Generate actionable reports or output.

The first step in the process is capturing raw transactional data points. Traditionally, the data is available in the form of plain text log files, which are usually analyzed and processed in one go. Even though it is easier for us to access and process information directly from a log file, it isn't advisable to do so. Before analyzing the data, we need to process the information from a log file into another medium, creating an additional step. Furthermore, an inherent problem with log processing is that it is difficult to do real-time analysis over the data as they are batch processed.

Capturing data in Redis

Let's assume that we are developing an online deals site such as http://slickdeals. net, which provides the best deals available online. We have hundreds of live deals on the site. The objective is to calculate the popularity of each deal. As the deals are usually short-lived, we want to calculate real-time popularity using Redis. Let's see how to use Redis to achieve this requirement.

Assume that the popularity of the deal is calculated using the number of times the deal was seen by the user and the number of times the user clicked on the link to go to the relevant store to claim the deal. Each of these actions has a weight of 1 and 5 respectively.

We will use sorted sets on each of the data points. In this case, we will be looking at two data points. On every visit, we will increment the score of the deal in deals:visits by one and on every link click, we will increment the score of the deal in deals:click by one.

For example, if a user visits the page of deal with ID 453, increment the visit count of the deal ID by executing the following command:

```
ZINCRBY deals:visits 1 "dealid:453"
```

Similarly, when the user visits other deals, we will increment the score for the respective deal ID as follows:

```
ZINCRBY deals:visits 1 "dealid:282"
ZINCRBY deals:visits 1 "dealid:453"
ZINCRBY deals:visits 1 "dealid:1169"
ZINCRBY deals:visits 1 "dealid:453"
ZINCRBY deals:visits 1 "dealid:282"
```

ZINCRBY key increment member

This increments the score of the member in the sorted set stored at key by increment. If a member does not exist in the sorted set, it is added with an increment as its score (as if its previous score was 0.0). If a key does not exist, a new sorted set with the specified member as its sole member is created. For more information, visit http://redis.io/commands/zincrby.

We can do the same for link clicks:

```
ZINCRBY deals:clicks 1 "dealid:453"
ZINCRBY deals:clicks 1 "dealid:282"
```

Analysis of data

To analyze the top deals based on page views, we can use ZREVRANGE, which gives us a view of all the required data:

```
> ZREVRANGE deals:visits 0 -1 WITHSCORES
1) "dealid:453"
2) 3.0
3) "dealid:282"
4) 2.0
5) "dealid:1169"
6) 1.0
```

> **ZREVRANGE**
>
> This returns the specified range of elements in the sorted set stored at key. The elements are considered to be ordered from the highest to the lowest score. Descending lexicographical order is used for elements with equal score. For more information, visit, http:// redis.io/commands/zrevrange.

In case we want to look into pages that have at least two views, we can use the following command:

```
> ZREVRANGEBYSCORE deals:visits +inf 2
1) "dealid:453"
2) "dealid:282"
```

We can get the click-through data in a similar manner:

```
> ZREVRANGE deals:clicks 0 -1 WITHSCORES
1) "dealid:453"
2) 1.0
3) "dealid:282"
4) 1.0
```

Let's suppose that we want to compute the popularity of each of the deals based on visits and clicks. Here, ZUNIONSTORE comes in handy.

ZUNIONSTORE destination numkeys key [key ...] [WEIGHTS weight [weight ...]] [AGGREGATE SUM | MIN | MAX]

This computes the union of numkeys sorted sets given by the specified keys, and stores the result in destination. For more information about ZUNIONSTORE, visit http://redis.io/commands/zunionstore.

```
> ZUNIONSTORE deals:pops 2 deals:visits deals:clicks WEIGHTS 1 5
(integer) 3
> ZREVRANGE deals:pops 0 -1 WITHSCORES
1) "dealid:453"
2) "8"
3) "dealid:282"
4) "7"
5) "dealid:1169"
6) "1"
```

If you see the scores in our deals:pops key, it is the sum of scores of deals:visits and deals:clicks multiplied by the weights we gave to ZUNIONSTORE. This information can be used to provide the real-time popularity of deals based on the user data. Overall, all of this can be achieved in under a few hundred lines of code. Adding another data point for our popularity logic is as simple as capturing the data in another sorted set and adding the sorted set into the ZUNIONSTORE command.

Session management and analysis using Redis

Sessions allow the web application to maintain the state across multiple requests. There are times when we need to store a lot of real-time session data. Saving the session data in a cookie is not always the best approach. So, it makes sense to move from cookie-based management to server-side session management. There is no limit to the amount of data we can store as session data. Typically, session data is stored in a temporary directory and the same variables are read on subsequent requests.

Why use Redis

If we have to use a load balancer with multiple web servers behind it, we need to centralize the session information. If not, we will end up having an inconsistent experience for the user. Let's say that the first request from the user was directed to server A, which then created the required session variables. If the subsequent request is directed to Server B by the load balancer, the session variables are lost and will be initialized again.

To solve this, we need to create a centralized session database. We can use MySQL or any relational database for the purpose, but writing and retrieving session information from MySQL is very slow and this is not acceptable for busy websites in most cases.

We can use memcached, which increases the performance. The problem with memcached is a lack of persistence. Also, in the case of an outage, you lose all the users' session information. This can be mitigated by configuring persistence in Redis. Redis, with its disk persistence support and ultrafast write and read rates, is ideally suited to solve the problem of centralized session data store. If the session data is critical, use *appendfsync always*. If losing a second of data is fine, consider using *appendfsync everysec* for persistence. This is how the process flows:

1. User requests would be received by the world-facing load balancer.

2. The load balancer allocates which web server serves the request among multiple web server instances.

3. All web servers use a common Redis instance or cluster as the session store.

4. As the entire array of web servers are connected to the same session data store in Redis, the session data is shared among all of them.

5. Even if one server goes down or is taken down for maintenance, session data is intact and will be served from other instances, thereby providing a superior experience to the users.

Session management using Redis is programming language agnostic. However, all the major programming languages or servers provide libraries and bindings to support Redis for session management. Most of them feature in-built functionality or can be enabled through third-party integration. Depending on the programming language and server used, the configuration of the session store varies.

The main advantage of using Redis is the ability to perform real-time data analysis over the session data. For example, we can store the number of pages visited by the user in the session variable. As the data is in Redis, the processing of data can be done with little effort. Information such as the number of visitors to the website and session duration can also be processed out of Redis.

Summary

In this chapter, we discussed real-time data analysis for a deals website, and also the benefits of using Redis as a session data store. While what we have covered as part of this chapter is minimal, it should give you an idea of what can be achieved with Redis. Redis as a data structure is flexible enough that we can plug it into any kind of system and take advantage of ultrafast access rates and extensibility. In the next chapter, we will see how to use Redis for managing leaderboards and also look at another little-known feature called publish/subscribe.

8
Redis in Gaming

The gaming industry thrives on the competitive nature of the human mind. Social gaming is another dimension where we, as players, can compete with other players across the world. Ranking of players based on score or skill is very common in any social game. This creates the necessary competition among friends and increases the engagement of the player in the game. So, leaderboards improve the motivation of the user to play or engage with the system. Apart from the leaderboards, real-time multiplayer games also take advantage of the notification system where an action performed by one of the players triggers a notification for another user. This could be as simple as notifying a user when another player has moved a piece in an online chess game, a city has been attacked in a virtual medieval simulation game, or your friend has beaten your highest score.

In *Chapter 7*, *Redis in Real-time Analysis*, we learned about using Redis in real-time. The capability to analyze data on the go makes more sense in the gaming industry. In this chapter, we will discuss the following areas:

- How to make leaderboards in Redis
- The notification center using publish/subscribe

Leaderboards in Redis

Leaderboards are common not only in gaming platforms, but also in online communities and Q&A sites where gamification can lead to better user engagement. It is a well-proven concept that gamification improves engagement. If you have played any online games on your mobile, you will already be familiar with how the games use leaderboards and rank the players based on various parameters. In this section, we will see how to create a simple leaderboard.

Check out the leaderboard in www.amazon.com for top reviewers (https://www.amazon.com/review/top-reviewers). Reddit has a leaderboard for links at http://www.reddit.com/top/.

If you have not guessed yet, we will be using a sorted set. Assume that we have a game where the user collects stars and scores points based on time. Now, we want to make two leaderboards based on the collected stars and game points of the players. The leaderboard score is based on the highest score by the player till that moment, while the collected star is the cumulative sum of all the stars collected by the player.

Whenever the user completes a game, we will add or update the information to the sorted set. The score leaderboard is lb:points, and our player ID is p:453. The player has scored 1169 points and has collected eight stars. Now, type the following commands:

```
ZADD lb:points 1169 p:453
ZINCRBY lb:stars 8 p:453
```

Notice that we have used ZADD for scores and ZINCRBY for stars. If the member already exists, ZADD updates the score. In the case of ZINCRBY, the score is incremented. If the member does not exist, a member is created and incremented from zero. This helps us execute the commands without the need to check whether the player already exists in our leaderboard, thereby keeping the system simple.

All the players who complete the game need to be added to the same sorted set. Now, to see the top five players based on points, type the following command:

```
ZREVRANGEBYSCORE lb:points +INF -INF withscores LIMIT 0 5
```

The preceding command will return the top five users and the respective points in a descending order by points.

ZREVRANGEBYSCORE key max min [WITHSCORES] [LIMIT offset count]

The time complexity is $O(log(N)+M)$, with N being the number of elements in the sorted set and M the number of elements that are returned. If M is constant, it is $O(log(N))$. For more information, visit http://redis.io/commands/ZREVRANGEBYSCORE.

In the case of our leaderboard, we want to paginate the results and show the next top five players. For this, type the following command:

```
ZREVRANGEBYSCORE lb:points +INF -INF withscores LIMIT 5 5
```

The same commands, when executed on lb:stars, will provide the leaderboard for the total number of stars that have been collected.

If you want to see the individual user details, you can fetch the values from the same set. Using the following commands, we can create a scorecard for individual users, if required. Assuming that we have inserted more users into the system and now our user p:453 is ranking at the fourteenth place, type the following command:

```
ZREVRANK lb:points p:453
14
ZSCORE lb:points p:453
"1169"
```

Now, we have discussed how to create a simple leaderboard based on a single data point. If we want to create another leaderboard based on a combination of both the user score points and collected stars, we can use ZUNIONSTORE.

> To find out more about the ZUNIONSTORE command, visit http://redis.io/commands/zunionstore.

Now, we want to create a global dashboard for all the players with a combination of points and stars. Assuming that each star is five times more valuable than the score point, type the following command:

```
ZUNIONSTORE lb:global 2 lb:points lb:stars WEIGHTS 1 5 AGGREGATE SUM
```

After the preceding command, we can use the following command to get the top five players:

```
ZREVRANGEBYSCORE lb:global +INF -INF withscores LIMIT 0 5
```

To get the individual rank of a player, use the following command:

```
ZREVRANK lb:global p:45317
```

The notification center

Notification systems are used a lot in any gaming system, especially in multiplayer social gaming. Notifications play a vital role in notifying the user about certain events in the game. For example, let's say we are developing an online chess game portal where two human players can play real time against each other on our website. It is important to notify the user about the moves of another user and remind them that it is their turn to move the piece.

The problem statement

We want to achieve the following results in a chess game between player A and player B:

- After any move from player A, player B should be notified about their turn

- In real time, player A and player B should be allowed to chat

- In real time, other players (spectators) can also subscribe to the game and participate in the chat

- The spectators can enter or leave the game at any time

To solve this situation, we will see how the publish/subscribe feature in Redis works and how to use it.

Publish/subscribe

Redis implements the publish/subscribe messaging paradigm. Redis, with its off-the-chart performance, can be used to implement a real-time messaging system. The concept of pub/sub is simple and works as follows:

- Publishers create a channel with a name

- Subscribers who are interested in certain channels subscribe to any number of channels

- Publishers can push messages into the channel without any knowledge about who might be listening to the message

- All the subscribers to the channels receive the message that they have subscribed to without any knowledge about the publisher

To know more about pub/sub, visit `http://redis.io/topics/pubsub`.

This completely decouples the publishers and subscribers, allowing for more scalability and dynamic network topology. Now, we will see how to use pub/sub to solve the notification system for our new online chess game.

The solution overview

As soon as a chess game starts, we can create a channel with the game name and subscribe to the channel. The following SUBSCRIBE command is used to subscribe to a channel:

```
SUBSCRIBE game:1
```

SUBSCRIBE channel [channel ...]

The time complexity is *O(N)*, where *N* is the number of channels to subscribe to. The SUBSCRIBE channel [channel ...] command subscribes the client to the specified channels. To find out more, visit http://redis.io/commands/subscribe.

Once the client enters the subscribed state, no other commands can be issued except other publish/subscribe related commands. The SUBSCRIBE command needs to be provided by both player A and player B. Now both players are listening to the channel. If anyone publishes any message to the channel, both players will receive the message.

For player A or B to publish a message to the channel, another connection needs to be made to Redis. As we want to receive and send messages from the same users, we need to have two connections per user—one as the publisher and another as the subscriber.

On successful subscription, we receive the following response from the server:

```
1) "subscribe"
2) "game:1"
3) (integer) 1
```

Now the game starts; after any specific move by player A, player A publishes a status into the game:1 channel using the PUBLISH command. The PUBLISH command pushes the message into the mentioned channel:

```
PUBLISH game:1 "Player A - MOVE - e2e4"
```

Now, subscribed clients of both player A and player B will receive the following message:

```
1) "message"
2) "game:1"
3) "Player A - MOVE - e2e4"
```

The received message says that it is from player A and notifies player B about the move taken by the user. So, the subscribed client of player B can show a visual notification about the move, reminding the player about their turn to play. If we want to send more details, such as check or checkmate, we can send them in a message. We are free to send any message, and both the players will receive the message:

```
PUBLISH game:1 "Player B - CHECK"

(integer) 2
```

Both player A and B receive the following messages:

```
1) "message"
2) "game:1"
3) "Player B - CHECK"
```

Now, for spectators, all the spectators should subscribe to the same channel. Since we want the spectators to only view the game and not allow them to publish messages in the channel, we need to create only one Redis subscriber client:

```
SUBSCRIBE game:1
1) "subscribe"
2) "game:1"
3) (integer) 1
```

Once subscribed, the spectator receives all the messages transmitted by both player A and player B.

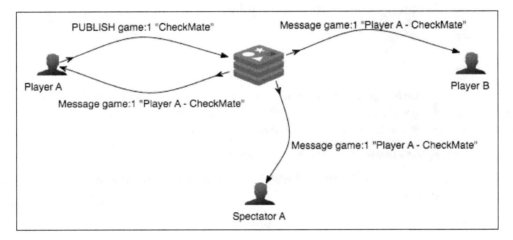

Whenever the spectator wants to stop updates from game:1, he can unsubscribe from the channel using the UNSUBSCRIBE command:

```
UNSUBSCRIBE game:1
1) "unsubscribe"
2) "game:1"
3) (integer) 0
```

To implement chatting between the players, we can use the same channel or a different channel, based on our requirements. If we want to allow spectators to view the chat messages, we can use the same channel or use a different channel if we want the chat to be private for players:

```
PUBLISH game:1 "Player A - Nice Move there."
```

Everyone who has an active subscription to the channel will receive the following messages:

```
1)  "message"

2)  "game:1"

3)  "Player A - Nice Move there."
```

Now, if any player wants to leave the game, we just need to use the UNSUBSCRIBE message. This command lets the user stop listening to a channel.

To really understand the flexibility of the system, we will add another requirement.

We want to log every message transmitted as part of a game so that the players can analyze the game later. This will come handy if we want to add a feature such as game replay.

This can be accomplished easily by automatically creating a subscriber who receives the message and logs the information into some kind of data store for every game created. We can also use the PSUBSCRIBE command to subscribe to all channels that match a pattern.

PSUBSCRIBE pattern [pattern ...]

The time complexity is $O(N)$, where N is the number of patterns the client has already subscribed to and subscribes the client to the given patterns. To find out more, check http://redis.io/commands/psubscribe.

The following command allows you to subscribe to all the channels that start with "game:". In short, it subscribes to all the games that are currently active:

```
PSUBSCRIBE game:*
```

As you can see, we can create a powerful yet flexible messaging system easily using Redis. While pub/sub fits very well into the messaging or notification system, this is not the only use case. The publish/subscribe messaging paradigm can be used in real-time monitoring systems and also in asynchronous event logging.

Summary

In this chapter, we saw how to use Redis to build a leaderboard and how to rank players based on multiple data points. We also designed a notification system using the publish/subscribe messaging paradigm. In the next chapter, we will discuss how to use Redis to develop a fast and responsive commenting system.

Redis in a Commenting System

9

In this chapter, we will look at how to use Redis as the primary data store. In particular, we will see how to design a commenting system using Redis.

Most of the content-management systems provide some form of user-commenting system to capture user feedback. Any basic commenting system includes the ability to post comments, and store and display the user-submitted comments along with the normal blog content. Redis, being a flexible data store, provides many different approaches for storing comments, depending on our product design. In this section, let's see different implementation details and trade-offs of each option.

 `https://muut.com/` is a forum/commenting system that uses Redis as the primary data store and to serve the 1,000 API calls for serving comments and still is able to fulfill API calls within two seconds.

A nonthreaded comment system

A nonthreaded comment system is really old school these days, where the comments are always provided to the main content of the page. The user cannot provide a reply to comments made by other users. We will see how to implement a simple nonthreaded system followed by the threaded comments that need a few architectural requirements.

Consider that we want to store the following information for any comment:

- **Comment ID**: This is a unique ID for comments in our system
- **Author**: This is the name of the user who has posted the comment

- **Comment text**: This is the full text of the comment along with any styling the user has provided
- **Comment timestamp**: This is the time when the comment was posted
- **URL Slug**: This is the URL link to the comment in case we want to link comments

Posting a new comment

Apart from this information related to comments, we should be able to find the post for which the comments were made. As this is a nonthreaded comment system, we can use lists to store the comment IDs for each post and store the comments in hashes:

```
LPUSH post:121:comments comment:4

HMSET comment:4 author "John Smith" text "Very informative post"
timestamp "2014-05-17 23:00:34" Slug "/comment/4"
```

LPUSH key value [value ...]

The time complexity is *O(1)*. Insert all the specified values at the head of the list stored at the key. If the key does not exist, it is created as an empty list before performing the push operations. When the key holds a value that is not a list, an error is returned. For more details, visit http://redis.io/commands/lpush.

The commands above can be used to create a comment object for a post.

Updating an existing comment

In case we want to update an existing comment, we can only update the hashes without updating the set:

```
HMSET comment:4 author "John Smith" text "Very informative post but can
be better." timestamp "2014-05-17 23:07:28" Slug "/comment/4"
```

HMSET key field value [field value ...]

This sets the specified fields to their respective values in the hash stored at the key. This command overwrites any existing fields in the hash. If the key does not exist, a new key holding a hash is created. For examples and details, check http://redis.io/commands/hmset.

In order to delete a comment from the system, we need to delete it from both sets and also the hashes. Even though deleting the member from a set will suffice, it is necessary to delete it from the hashes in order to avoid ghost keys that stay in Redis without any reference to them:

```
DEL comment:4
```

```
LREM post:121:comments 0 comment:4
```

 To find out more about LREM, visit `http://redis.io/commands/lrem`.

Displaying the comments

Assuming we have not deleted the comment in the previous section, to retrieve the comments for any post, we only need to know the post ID:

```
LRANGE post:121:comments 0 -1
```

```
1) "comment:4"
```

Now, iterate through all the members and fetch the comment hashes to display the information:

```
HGETALL comment:4
```

```
1) "author"
```

```
2) "John Smith"
```

```
3) "text"
```

```
4) "Very informational post but can be better"
```

```
5) "timestamp"
```

```
6) "2014-05-17 23:07:28"
```

```
7) "Slug"
```

```
8) "/comment/4"
```

In order to paginate the comments, we can use LRANGE to fetch only a specific number of comments from the list using the start and stop parameters of LRANGE.

```
LRANGE post:121:comments 0 10
```

The preceding command will give 10 comments for the post starting from the latest comment. To get the next set of 10 comments, use the following command:

```
LRANGE post:121:comments 10 10
```

LRANGE key start stop

$O(S+N)$, where S is the start offset and N is the number of elements in the specified range. For more information, visit http://redis.io/commands/lrange.

Threaded comments

In order to support threaded comments, we need to change the structure a little bit. We need to start storing the ID of the parent comment as parent_id for the comments, which are replies to existing comments. We will use the lists and hashes to store the comments. Instead of a single list per post, we will use multiple lists based on whether the comment is a child of another comment or a parent comment.

The following is the PHP code snippet that stores threaded comments in Redis:

```php
function save_comment($post_id, $author, $comment, $parent_id = 0) {
  $isParent = false;
  if($parent_id === 0) {
    $isParent = false;
  }
  else {
    $isParent = true;
    $redis->hSet("comment:$parent_id", "hasChildren", 1);
  }

  $comment_data = array("comment_id" => $redis-
>incr("comments:id:next"),
    "parent_id" => $parent_id,
    "author" => $author,
    "text" => $comment,
    "post_id" => $post_id,
    "hasChildren" => 0,
    "time" => time());

  if($isParent) {
    $redis->rPush("post:" . $post_id . ":comments", $comment_
data['comment_id']);
  } else {
```

```
    $redis->rPush("thread:" . $parentId, $comment_data['comment_
id']);
    }

  $redis->hMSet("comment:" . $data['id'], $data);
    return $comment_data['comment_id'];
}
```

The preceding code snippet saves the comment in Redis based on the parameters passed to it. If the comment is not a reply to another comment, we save the comment ID in a list that contains all the master comments for the particular post ID.

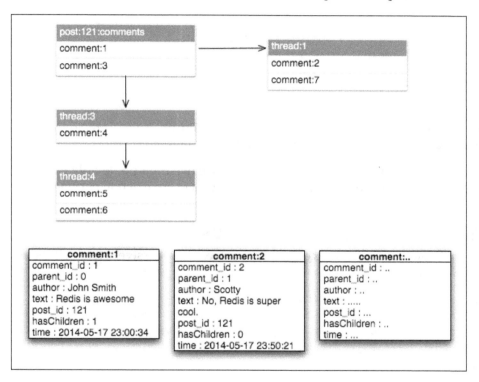

In this case, the comment is a reply to another comment; we store the comment threads in another list based on the parent ID of the comment. We also update the hasChildren field of the parent comment object. As usual the comment information is stored as hashes. We are using a comments:id:next key to maintain the auto increment ID value for the comment.

Updating or deleting a comment

In case we want to delete a comment for a post, it is necessary to delete all the children comments as well. We need to recursively find all the children and delete the lists along with the corresponding hashes. The following is the PHP code snippet that deletes threaded comments in Redis:

```php
function delete_comment ($comment_id) {
  $has_children = $redis->hmget("comment:$comment_id","hasChildren");
  if($has_children) {
    $comment_list = $redis->lrange("thread:$comment_id", 0, -1);
    foreach($comment_list as $comment) {
      delete_comment($comment);
    }
    $redis->del("thread:$comment_id");
  }
  $redis->del("comment:$comment_id");
}
```

The function checks whether the comment has children. If yes, it recursively deletes the comment thread and also deletes the comment object.

It is easier in the case of a comment update as we need to update only the hashes, and the comment tree need not be changed to update an existing comment.

Displaying a comment tree

Now, to display the threaded comments, we have to recursively fetch all the master comments and their children:

```php
function get_comments ($post_id) {
  $comment_data = get_comment_data("post:" . $post_id . ":comments");
  $parsed_comments = process_comment_tree($comment_data);
  return $parsed_comments;
}

function get_comment_data($key) {
  $comment_list = $redis->lrange($key, 0, -1);
  $comment_data = array();
  foreach($comment_list as $comment) {
    $comment_data[] = $redis->hgetall($comment);
  }
```

```
    return $comment_data;
}

function process_comment_tree ($comments) {
  $curr = array();
  foreach($comments as $comment) {
    if($comment['hasChildren'] === "1") {
      $data = get_comment_data("thread:" . $comment['comment_id']);
      $curr[$comment['comment_id']] = process_comment_tree($data);
    }
  $curr[$comment['parent_id']][] = $comment;
  }
  return $curr;
}
```

In the preceding functions, the `get_comments` function receives the `post_id` for which we wish to show the comments. It fetches the information about the comments from hashes using the `get_comment_data` function. Then, it executes `process_comment_tree` and recursively recreates the comment tree. The output of the program will be a multilevel array of comments made to that specific post.

> The output of the `get_comments` function can be cached in Redis as `post:121:processed_comment`. This reduces the processing required every time. The cache can be invalidated whenever a new comment is made from the `save_comment` function.

Let's add another requirement to our commenting system. We want to order the comments based on the number of up votes or number of replies each comment has got rather than based on time. If you have not guessed it already, sorted sets can be used to solve this problem. Instead of using a list to store the comments and children, sorted sets need to be used. The score field can be used to store the comment up votes.

Summary

In this chapter, we discussed how to use Redis to implement a simple yet sophisticated commenting system. If you wonder whether Redis can handle the load of creating a comment tree on every page view, you might find this blog post interesting: `https://muut.com/blog/technology/redis-as-primary-datastore-wtf.html`. In the next chapter, we will discuss a time-sensitive, advertisement serving system.

10
Redis in Advertising Networks

In this chapter, we will examine how to build an online advertising network using Redis. Advertising networks connect the advertisers and publisher websites. Advertisers provide the display ads along with a set of attributes for the ad that should be displayed. Publisher websites provide the content pages with regions marked for ad displays. When the page is displayed, the request is made to the ad network and relevant ads are shown in the designated ad slot.

Typically, an ad network tracks and records the number of page views, the number of times each ad is displayed, the number of clicks on ads, and other statistics that are required to optimize and bill the advertiser.

The key performance criteria for an ad-serving network is based on the time taken from receiving a request to returning a targeted advertisement to be displayed. Redis, being blazingly fast, is well suited for this requirement.

We will start with the basic algorithm for serving the ad, and then, we will progressively refine the solution to include more complex scenarios such as keyword targeting and optimization.

The basic steps are as follows:

1. The network receives a request from a website with its `website_id` and `slot_id` for which the ad is to be served.
2. The network searches in its ad catalog, which contains all active ad campaigns, and chooses the best ad based on business rules.
3. The network sends the ad to be displayed and implements a view for the ad.

For the system to work, we need to have a collection of ads in our system along with `website_id` and `slot_id` received as part of our request. In a later part of the chapter, we will discuss more advanced targeting.

For simplicity, `slot_id` will be of these types: banner, skyscraper, and square ad blocks. In order to store the different ads, we will use the sorted set for each type, ordered and based on its **effective cost per mile (eCPM)** values.

Advertising jargon

In this chapter, ad networks make decisions about what ads to serve, and these decisions will be based on eCPM. This is a measure that lets us draw a comparison between **cost per mile (CPM)** ads, which are priced based on the number of impressions, and **cost per click (CPC)** ads, which are priced per click. The eCPM of a CPM ad is just the CPM. In the case of a CPC ad, the calculation of eCPM is based on the **click-through rate (CTR)**, which is defined as the number of clicks per ad impression. The formula for calculating the eCPM for a CPC ad is as follows:

$$eCPM = CPC \times CTR \times 1000$$

In our case, consider that we know the eCPM for all the ad blocks. In real-world ad networks, we need to calculate the eCPM and store it for processing.

The ad inventory

We will create a sorted set for each type of ads (`slot_id`) and the sorted set will contain `ad_id`, which will be assigned to any ad that is added to the system ordered by the eCPM value for that ad:

```
ZADD slot:banner 2.25 ad:1
ZADD slot:banner 4.75 ad:2
ZADD slot:banner 1.65 ad:3
```

Other information related to the ad will be stored as hashes. The information includes `campaign_id` and the ad snippet to be served. We will add more information related to the ad in this hash:

```
HMSET ad:1 campaign_id 100 slot_id banner ad_snippet {html-fragment}
HMSET ad:2 campaign_id 100 slot_id banner ad_snippet {html-fragment}
HMSET ad:3 campaign_id 101 slot_id banner ad_snippet {html-fragment}
```

A single campaign can have multiple ad units. In order to manage the status of the campaign, we can create a set that will contain all the `ad_id` belonging to that campaign:

```
SADD campaign:100 ad:1 ad:2
SADD campaign:101 ad:3
```

Choosing the best ad to serve

Now, when a request comes in with `website_id` and `slot_id`, we need to process the request and then decide what is the most compatible ad to serve that request while also maximizing the eCPM for that request.

We will pick the top ads ordered by the eCPM and also pick the ad with the highest eCPM to be shown on the publisher's site. However, the problem with using this method is that the same ad is delivered every time to the website, which is not preferred by the advertiser. For now, we will deliver an ad randomly. Once advanced targeting and frequency capping comes into play, the logic to choose an ad will get complex. The following command on execution will give the ad unit, which has maximum eCPM:

```
ZREVRANGEBYSCORE slot:banner +inf -inf LIMIT 0 1
```

ZREVRANGEBYSCORE key max min [WITHSCORES] [LIMIT offset count]

This returns all the elements in the sorted set at the key with a score between maximum and minimum (including elements with scores equal to maximum or minimum). Contrary to the default ordering of sorted sets, the elements for this command are considered to be ordered from high to low scores. For more information, visit `http://redis.io/commands/zrevrangebyscore`.

Once we decide which `ad_id` needs to be rendered, we can get the details from the respective hashes and send the details back to the website. In order to be able to provide the performance information relating to the ad, such as CTR, the number of impressions, and other metrics, we need to know how many times a particular ad unit is delivered.

Pausing or stopping a campaign

In order to stop or pause a campaign, all we need to do is remove the ad from the respective slot's sorted set. To stop `campaign:100`, type the following command:

```
SMEMBERS campaign:100
1) ad:1
2) ad:2
```

Now, iterate through `ad_ids`, and remove the ad from the selection pool:

```
ZREM slot:banner ad:1 ad:2
```

From the next request, the ad units as part of the specific campaign will not be delivered to the websites.

Frequency capping

In our previous solution, there was a possibility of the same ad being shown to the same user over and over again until the budget was exhausted as we deliver in order to maximize eCPM for the website. To solve this issue in the advertising world, the advertiser is given the ability to limit the frequency with which the same user is presented with the same ad. This methodology is called frequency capping.

As frequency capping is based on the users, we need to maintain a data store to manage the user profile information, such as the impression count for each ad and conversion. The user_id will usually be maintained as a cookie in the user's browser in order to track the user across the session. Every time a request for an ad comes to the network, the user_id from the cookie is used in the ad-serving decision.

Impression information for a user should be stored per campaign in order to make sure that the ad from the same campaign is not shown every time. This can be achieved with the help of the following commands:

```
INCR user:id1:campaign:100
INCR user:id1:campaign:101
INCR user:id2:campaign:102
```

Every time an ad is served to the user, we increment the impression count for that particular user and for that campaign. Also, we will store the frequency capping for each campaign provided by the advertiser.

Selecting an ad with frequency capping

Now, instead of picking the top ad with the maximum eCPM, we need to iterate through the ad units ordered by the eCPM and find the best possible ad based on the frequency capping. To do so, perform the following steps:

1. Fetch all the ad units available for the particular slot id by typing the following command:

    ```
    ZREVRANGEBYSCORE slot:banner +inf -inf
    ```

2. Iterate through the ad units and check whether the user has reached the capping limit for that campaign yet:

    ```
    HGET ad:1 campaign_id
    1) 100
    GET user:id1:campaign:100
    ```

3. If the user has already reached the limit, continue the iteration; else, deliver the ad snippet to the website and increment the impression count for that user to the particular campaign.

 We need to expire the impression count after a certain time limit, as frequency capping is usually time-bound. To achieve this, the EXPIRE function of Redis comes in handy. By setting the expiry to user:id1:campaign:100, we will achieve the desired behavior. To find out more about the expire command, visit http://redis.io/commands/expire.

Keyword targeting

Keyword targeting is another important feature for any advertising network. Advertisers would like to show their advertisements on related websites where the audience of the website closely matches their target audience. While frequency capping is an example of user-based targeting, keyword targeting is more about targeting a related website.

Large ad networks crawl web pages to match the page contents with the target keywords provided by the advertisers. For the sake of simplicity, we will consider ad targeting based on the search keyword provided by the user in the website and will match only the exact matches of a keyword.

To accommodate keyword targeting in our system, we need to store the keywords provided by the advertisers for each of the campaigns. In order to improve the real-time performance, we will create a reverse index for the keywords and store the campaign IDs as members of the keywords.

For example, keywords for the campaigns are as follows:

*   Campaign_100 - android, phones, holo design
*   Campaign_101 - windows, phones, flat design

Now, we will store the information as a reverse index in Redis:

```
SADD android campaign:100
SADD phones campaign:100 campaign:101
SADD "holo design" campaign:100
SADD "flat design" campaign:101
```

To add or remove the keyword from a campaign, we need to remove the campaign ID from the keyword in the set or add it. To add the material design as the keyword to the campaign, run the following command:

```
SADD "material design" campaign:100
```

To remove `holo design` from the keyword list of a campaign, run the following command:

```
SREM "holo design" campaign:100
```

Selecting an ad based on keyword targeting

Now, let's see how to deliver the ad with keyword targeting in effect. We will extend the previous solution of frequency capping and perform the following steps:

1. Once the request comes in with the keyword (phones), we will fetch all the campaigns applicable for the keyword by typing the following command:

   ```
   SMEMBERS phones
   1) campaign:100
   2) campaign:101
   ```

2. We will get all the ad units that are relevant, based on the keyword targeting with the help of the following command:

   ```
   SUNION campaign:100 campaign:101
   ```

   The preceding command will unite all the ad units that are available as part of both the campaigns.

    SUNION key [key ...]
   This returns the members of the set resulting from the union of all the given sets. For examples, check `http://redis.io/commands/sunion`.

3. We will fetch all the ad units applicable for the particular `slot_id`, the same as we did earlier, by typing the following command:

   ```
   ZREVRANGEBYSCORE slot:banner +inf -inf
   ```

4. Before we start iterating, we will perform the following operation:

    ○ Intersect the two lists that we have from step 2 and step 3 to get all the ad units matching both the keyword targeting and the slot ID

    ○ Now, iterate through each ad unit id

    ○ Get the campaign ID of the ad unit from the hash of the ad unit

    ○ Check the user frequency for the particular campaign. If the frequency capping limit is not met, deliver the ad unit. Else, continue with the iteration

The ad unit delivered earlier will meet all the targeting parameters, including frequency capping.

 We assume that all keywords are of equal importance, which is not usually the case in real-life situations. In case we want to match multiword search terms, we can perform the union of the keywords in order to find the campaigns that match most of the keywords.

Summary

In this chapter, we built a very basic ad delivery network using Redis. Though this is not even close to what is required in a real advertising network, it should provide you with some ideas on how Redis can be used in a few features of an ad network in order to make the system faster. A few complex cases of targeting might get very complex to be implemented in Redis; however, maintaining the indexes in Redis helps in speeding up the ad delivery considerably. In the next chapter, we will see how Redis is well suited to implementing some exciting features in social networks.

11
Redis in Social Networks

In this chapter, we will explore various features where Redis can be effectively used in a social network. Redis is being used in leading social networking sites such as Twitter, Instagram, Flickr, Quora, and Stack Overflow to maintain social relationships or to generate dynamic news feeds for users.

> You can read how Pinterest uses Redis to maintain its social graph at `http://engineering.pinterest.com/post/55272557617/building-a-follower-model-from-scratch`.

In this chapter, we will cover the following topics:

- Building a simple social network with authentication
- Designing friendship circles
- Handling posts and news feeds in our social network

Building your own social network

In this section, we will build a simple social network using Redis as the backend. We will also see how to design a social graph defining the social interactions or relationships between the users. A social graph is used to show the relationships between the users of your application or website. This is important, as the users are the integral part of a social network. To keep the system simple for the purposes of this book, we will store the following information for a user: e-mail address, location, gender, and age.

Storing user information

What information should be stored for a user depends on the kind of social network we want to build. In the case of a personal social network, information such as relationship status, interests, and others are important, whereas in the case of professional networks, educational details, work experience, and skills are more relevant. For this chapter, we will store basic information such as age, location, gender, and e-mail address for our users. In the following commands, we will have a global key named `nextUid` to create an auto incremented unique ID for every user:

```
INCR gbl:nextUid
1000
```

```
SET uid:1000:email john.smith@packtpub.com
SET uid:1000:password d41d8cd98f00b204e9800998ecf8427e
```

In preceding commands, we have created two keys, one with the e-mail ID and another key with the hashed password for a particular user. Always use a strong hashing algorithm along with salt before storing the password.

For the login, we need to get the user ID from the e-mail ID of the user. To easily get the user ID from an e-mail ID instead of iterating all the keys, we need to create another reverse lookup key in Redis as follows:

```
SET email:john.smith@packtpub.com:uid 1000
```

We can store other information such as age, gender, and location of the user, which we will not use to look up, as hashes:

```
HMSET uid:1000:info email john.smith@packtpub.com age 30 gender M
location "New York"
```

We have a global key, `nextUid`, which is used to increment and assign a user ID to new users. All information about the user will be accessed using the user ID.

Authenticating a user

User authentication is critical in any social networking application to maintain privacy and to avoid misuse of user accounts. Though the level of sophistication and security to be provided for the user authentication depends on the application, we will see the basic steps to perform user authentication:

1. Check if the e-mail exists in our system by retrieving the user ID for the e-mail ID:

    ```
    GET email:john.smith@packtpub.com:uid
    1000
    ```

2. If the user ID does not exist, we will create a new user with the e-mail ID and newly incremented value of `gbl:nextUid`.

3. If the user ID exists, we will validate the password provided by the user by typing the following command:

    ```
    GET uid:1000:password
    ```

4. If the password matches, log in the user using the authentication method of your application, such as cookie-based or session-based authentication.

Building a relationship with the user

In our social network, we will allow people to add other people as friends. However, the friendship request needs to be accepted before the friendship relationship can be established between two users. In order to maintain the friendship, we need to maintain three sets for each user, one for received friend requests, a second one for all accepted friends, and a third one for all sent friend requests.

Adding a friend

To send a new friend request to a user, we will add the user ID of the requesting user into the set. For example, if a user with ID 1000 wants to add a user with ID 453 as a friend, we will add the user ID 1000 into the friend request set of user 453 as follows:

```
SADD uid:453:requests 1000
```

Also, we need to maintain all the relationships in a bidirectional manner. In order to show all the pending friend requests, we need to have a set for requested users as well. To do so, run the following command:

```
SADD uid:1000:pendingrequests 453
```

Now, to show all the new friend requests received by any user, we just need to get the list of user IDs from the set and show these to the user. To show the new friend requests to user 453, we will execute SMEMBERS on the `uid:453:requests` key and show the user's information.

Accepting a friend request

Once the user accepts the friend request, we need to add the user ID to the friends list of both the users. If a user with ID 453 accepts the friend request from the user with ID 1000, we will run the following commands:

```
SADD uid:1000:friendslist 453
SADD uid:453:friendslist 1000
SREM uid:453:requests 1000
SREM uid:1000:pendingrequests 453
```

In the case where the user rejects the friend request, we will only delete the request from the user's set and skip adding to the friends list as follows:

```
SREM uid:453:requests 1000
```

To avoid the racing condition in which two users send friend requests to each other at the same time, we need to check user 1's request queue before adding user 1's ID into user 2's request queue. If user 2's ID already exists in user 1's request queue, we will make the users friends. As Redis is atomic and single threaded, both the keys cannot be added at the same time and the previous check will avoid the racing condition.

Unfriending a user

If a user wants to unfriend another user, the operation is simple. We need to remove the ID of the users from each other's `friendslist` set as follows:

```
SREM uid:1000:friendslist 453
SREM uid:453:friendslist 1000
```

 Whenever there is more than one command to be executed as a single atomic command, it is advisable to use transactions to avoid any inconsistencies in the data. For more information about transactions in Redis, check http://redis.io/topics/transactions.

Updating posts and status

In a real-world social network, depending on the type of network, various kinds of activities such as status updates, photos, links, and videos are allowed. However, for this section, we will restrict activity types to posts and status updates only. The way posts and status updates are handled is identical. So, we will store status updates as posts in Redis.

The basic steps to be performed when someone is creating a new post are as follows:

1. The post information is saved into hash.
2. The post ID is stored into the author's post list.
3. The post ID is also updated into the newsfeed list of all the friends of the person who created the post.

To create a new unique post ID every time, we will use a global key like we did earlier for the user ID:

```
INCR gbl:nextPostId
282
```

After getting the unique post ID, we will store the information related to the post in a hash as follows:

```
HMSET post:282 by 1000 content "Hi all" posted_at "2014-08-10 23:28:14"
```

Once the hash is created, we will push the post ID into the status list of the user who created it as follows:

```
LPUSH uid:1000:statuses 282
```

Also, we will push the status update to all the friends of the user. Using the SMEMBERS function, get all the friends of the user and iterate through each user and push the status update into their updates list:

```
SMEMBERS uid:1000:friendslist
```

```
LPUSH uid:453:updates 282
```

The following PHP code will explain the complete flow:

```
function AddNewPost ($uid, $message) {
  $postid = $redis->incr('gbl:nextPostId');
  $redis->hmset("post:$postid", "by", $uid, "content", $message,
"posted_at", time());
  $redis->lpush("uid:$uid:statuses", $postid);
  $friendslist = $redis->smembers("uid:$uid:friendslist");
  foreach ($friendslist as $friend) {
    $redis->lpush("uid:$friend:updates", $postid);
  }
}
```

Now, if the user wants to edit the post that is already created, the operation is simply a case of updating the hash values for the post using HSET. We can even add modified time as another value to our post data just in case we want to notify the users about last modified time of the post.

If the user deletes the post, it is important we not only remove the post ID from the user's list but also from all of their friends updates lists. Also, we can delete the hash for that post ID as shown in the following code snippet:

```
function DeletePost ($postid) {
  $uid = $redis->hget("post:$postid", "by");

  $redis->lrem("uid:$uid:statuses", 0, $postid);
  $friendslist = $redis->smembers("uid:$uid:friendslist");
  foreach ($friendslist as $friend) {
    $redis->lrem("uid:$friend:updates", 0, $postid);
  }

  $redis->del("post:$postid");
}
```

Status update feed

One of the most used features in any social network is the news feed or updates feed, the page containing all the status updates or posts from all the friends. Because we have already stored the updates for any user in the uid:{userid}:updates list, it is very straightforward to query and display the news feed for the user.

In our case, let's say user ID 453 wants to view all the updates from his friends, all we need to do is get the post ID's stored in the uid:453:updates list. We will iterate through the post IDs and show the details to the user as follows:

```
function GetMyPostUpdates ($uid, $start, $count) {
  $post_details = array();
  $postIds = $redis->lrange("uid:$uid:updates", $start, $start+
$count);
  foreach ($posts as $postId) {
    $post_details[$postId] = $redis->hgetall("post:$postId");
  }
  return $post_details;
}
```

The preceding function will receive the user ID and also the start and count values for paginating the news feed. After getting the post IDs from the list, we iterate through the post IDs and get the information from the post hash and return the two dimensional array of post details.

Similarly, whenever a user visits another user's profile page, we can show all the posts made by that user using the `uid:{userid}:statuses` list. We only need to make sure that the visitor who is trying to visit the user's page is already a friend. If not, we need to ask the visitor to add the user as friend before showing the status updates as follows:

```
function getUserUpdates ($uid, $page_uid, $start, $count) {
  //check whether the $uid is a friend of $page_uid
  if (!$redis->sismember("uid:$page_uid:friendslist", $uid)) {
    return "Not a friend. Please add as friend to see updates";
  }
  $post_details = array();
  $postIds = $redis->lrange("uid:$page_uid:statuses", $start, $start +
$count);
  foreach ($posts as $postId) {
    $post_details[$postId] = $redis->hgetall("post:$postId");
  }
  return $post_details;
}
```

Commenting on posts

Another important feature in any social network is allowing the users to comment on the posts made by other users. Comments are the most common action taken in a social network. Without comments, the whole social activity on the post does not exist. In this section, we will see what it takes to add a commenting feature to our posts.

Comments are attributes of posts so they need to be stored as a list corresponding to the post IDs. Like posts, we will store the information about comments in a hash as follows:

```
function AddNewComment ($postId, $comment, $uid) {
  $commentId = $redis->incr('gbl:nextCommentId');
  $redis->hmset("comment:$commentId", "by", $uid, "content",$comment,
"commented_at", time());
  $redis->lpush("post:$postId:comments", $commentId);
}
```

To edit a comment, we need to update the hash for the particular comment.

```
function EditComment ($commentId, $comment) {
  $redis->hmset("comment:$commentId", "content", $comment, "edited_
at", time());
}
```

To delete a comment, we need to delete the comment ID from the respective post comments list and also the hash for that comment as follows:

```
function DeleteComment ($commentId, $postId) {
  $redis->del("comment:$commentId");
  $redis->lrem("post:$postId:comments", $commentId);
}
```

To display comments, we need to query the list. As the list maintains the same order in which it was inserted, we can show the comments in the same order in which they were created. If we want to sort in the reverse chronological order, we can reverse the array in the implementation code:

```
function GetComments ($postId, $start, $count) {
  $comment_details = array();
  $commentIds = $redis->lrange("post:$postId:comments", $start, $start
+ $count);
  foreach ($commentIds as $commentId) {
    $comment_details[$commentId] = $redis-
>hgetall("comment:$commentId");
  }
  return $comment_details;
}
```

 This commenting system is only one level. If you want to implement multilevel threaded comments, refer to the *Threaded comments* section in *Chapter 9, Redis in a Commenting System*.

Summary

In this chapter, we saw how to build a simple social network. We discussed how to authenticate users and maintain friendship circles. We also discussed how to store posts and comments on posts.

Redis, being very fast at completing the requests, can be best suited for features such as news feeds and status updates. For example, Quora uses Redis to render the front page feeds. Though the system we have designed needs more features to become a fully featured social network, it should provide you with a fair idea about how to use Redis to build a simple social network with all the basic features. With Redis replication and Redis sentinel (under development), it is going to be easier to scale Redis across many machines without the shortcomings of using RAM as the primary storage.

Index

sets 17
sorted sets 17, 18
strings 16
URL 15

E

effective cost per mile (eCPM) values 66
EXPIRE command 19
expiry mechanism
reference link 19
expiry, Redis
about 16
reference link 16

F

faceted search
about 39
performing 39, 40
forum/commenting system
reference link 57
frequency capping
about 68
ad based on frequency capping,
selecting 68, 69

G

GET cache server 22-25
get_comment_data function 63
get_comments function 63

H

hashes 18
HMSET key field value [field value ...]
about 58
URL 58
HSCAN
reference link 29
HyperLogLog
about 19
URL 19

I

inventory management
about 29
solution overview 30-32

K

keyword targeting
about 69, 70
ad based on keyword targeting,
selecting 70, 71

L

leaderboards
about 49
creating 50, 51
reference link 50
LPUSH key value [value ...]
about 58
URL 58
LRANGE key start stop
URL 60
LREM
URL 59

M

memory optimization techniques
reference link 23
multiword phrase completion
about 37, 38
inherent challenges 37
search, performing in index 38, 39

N

nextUid 74
n-gram 34
nonthreaded comment system
architectural requisites 57
comments, displaying 59
existing comment, updating 58, 59
new comment, posting 58

Thank you for buying
Redis Applied Design Patterns

About Packt Publishing

Packt, pronounced 'packed', published its first book *"Mastering phpMyAdmin for Effective MySQL Management"* in April 2004 and subsequently continued to specialize in publishing highly focused books on specific technologies and solutions.

Our books and publications share the experiences of your fellow IT professionals in adapting and customizing today's systems, applications, and frameworks. Our solution based books give you the knowledge and power to customize the software and technologies you're using to get the job done. Packt books are more specific and less general than the IT books you have seen in the past. Our unique business model allows us to bring you more focused information, giving you more of what you need to know, and less of what you don't.

Packt is a modern, yet unique publishing company, which focuses on producing quality, cutting-edge books for communities of developers, administrators, and newbies alike. For more information, please visit our website: www.packtpub.com.

About Packt Open Source

In 2010, Packt launched two new brands, Packt Open Source and Packt Enterprise, in order to continue its focus on specialization. This book is part of the Packt Open Source brand, home to books published on software built around Open Source licenses, and offering information to anybody from advanced developers to budding web designers. The Open Source brand also runs Packt's Open Source Royalty Scheme, by which Packt gives a royalty to each Open Source project about whose software a book is sold.

Writing for Packt

We welcome all inquiries from people who are interested in authoring. Book proposals should be sent to author@packtpub.com. If your book idea is still at an early stage and you would like to discuss it first before writing a formal book proposal, contact us; one of our commissioning editors will get in touch with you.

We're not just looking for published authors; if you have strong technical skills but no writing experience, our experienced editors can help you develop a writing career, or simply get some additional reward for your expertise.

Responsive Web Design with HTML5 and CSS3

ISBN: 978-1-84969-318-9   Paperback: 324 pages

Learn responsive design using HTML5 and CSS3 to adapt websites to any browser or screen size

1. Everything needed to code websites in HTML5 and CSS3 that are responsive to every device or screen size.

2. Learn the main new features of HTML5 and use CSS3's stunning new capabilities, including animations, transitions, and transformations.

3. Real-world examples show how to progressively enhance a responsive design while providing fallbacks for older browsers.

Socket.IO Real-time Web Application Development

ISBN: 978-1-78216-078-6   Paperback: 140 pages

Build modern real-time web applications powered by Socket.IO

1. Understand the usage of various Socket.IO features such as rooms, namespaces, and sessions.

2. Secure the Socket.IO communication.

3. Deploy and scale your Socket.IO and Node.js applications in production.

4. A practical guide that quickly gets you up and running with Socket.IO.

Please check **www.PacktPub.com** for information on our titles

Node Cookbook

ISBN: 978-1-84951-718-8   Paperback: 342 pages

Over 50 recipes to master the art of asynchronous
server-side JavaScript using Node

1. Packed with practical recipes taking you
   from the basics to extending Node with
   your own modules.

2. Create your own web server to see Node's
   features in action.

3. Work with JSON, XML, WebSockets, and make
   the most of asynchronous programming.

Hadoop Real-World Solutions Cookbook

ISBN: 978-1-84951-912-0   Paperback: 316 pages

Realistic, simple code examples to solve problems
at scale with Hadoop and related technologies

1. Solutions to common problems when
   working in the Hadoop environment.

2. Recipes for (un)loading data, analytics,
   and troubleshooting.

3. In depth code examples demonstrating
   various analytic models, analytic solutions,
   and common best practices.

Please check **www.PacktPub.com** for information on our titles